INDIA'S DEMOCRACY
AND THE
COMMUNIST CHALLENGE

by

I. C. SHARMA
Ph.D.

Head of the Department of Philosophy
M. B. College, University of Udaipur
Rajasthan

Edited and Revised by

STANLEY M. DAUGERT
Ph.D.

Chairman of the Department of Philosophy
Western Washington State College

Johnsen Publishing Company
Lincoln, Nebraska 68501

India's Democracy and the Communist Challenge

Copyright 1967, by Johnsen Publishing Company

Library of Congress Catalog Card No. 67-29919.

Table of Contents

Editor's Note

As in the case of Dr. Sharma's *Ethical Philosophies of India* (Allen and Unwin, London; Johnsen Press, Nebraska, 1965) I have attempted chiefly to smooth out the prose for the benefit of Western readers to allow the work to be read easily and without the interruptions of what to modern American ears would be solecisms and inelegancies.

The Research Advisory Bureau of Western Washington State College and Mrs. Mary Sutterman assisted in typing and preparing the manuscript for the press. We are grateful to both for their work.

STANLEY M. DAUGERT

Western Washington State College
Bellingham, Washington

Prologue

This book is the result of my first visit to the United States as a visiting professor from September 1962 to September 1963. After contact with many and various groups of people all over the country, frequently as an invited speaker, I strongly felt the need of writing a book giving a factual account of various political, social and cultural problems of India to satisfy the curiosity of inquisitive Westerners interested in the maintainance of freedom in India and throughout the world.

My experience in the United States brought home to me the fact that much important information about India is unknown to the average man in America. Although there exists an enormous literature about Chinese and Japanese culture, religion and philosophy, knowledge about the cultural, social and political life of India, the largest democracy in the world today (from the point of view of population), is comparatively meager in the United States and is based mainly on information transmitted by British writers. It is a plain and simple fact that the British had vested interests in India at least until 1947, and that most British accounts about India were politically motivated to justify the occupation of India as a dependent colony. Soon after India became independent she got so engrossed in her domestic problems that she was unable to project her own image abroad and to contradict or correct all that had been prejudicially propagated by the erstwhile rulers of the great subcontinent. There is great need for information on various aspects of Indian life written by Indian scholars. It is highly desirable that such scholars, especially those who might visit the United States, come to realize that the genuine curiosity of the people of this great country has been unsatisfied owing to the unavailability of anything approaching adequate knowledge of the historical facts, and the political, social and economic currents and undercurrents in India.

Moreover, many Indian intellectuals are idealistic and remain so as long as they stay within their own borders. Realism dawns upon such intellectuals only when they visit foreign countries and come face to face with the people and the conditions prevailing in these countries. I have tried in this book to get rid of my own idealistic tendency and to present an objective account of the struggle of India's democracy against the communist challenge. I do not claim to have given an exhaustive account of all major events, nor do I feel that my interpretation is absolutely valid or prophetic, although many events which occurred months after the bulk of the manuscript was ready proved the validity of many of my interpretations. Since the subject matter concerns the destiny of a very large and important country, a destiny which depends upon political and economic changes all over the world, only a true prophet (assuming there is such) might draw absolutely necessary conclusions about the future. It will suffice here to say that looking to the general aptitude of the Indian people, totalitarianism of the communist type will not conquer India if the democratically inclined leaders of the nation adopt a realistic attitude and make honest efforts to educate the masses in making the best use of their franchise. If there is any danger to the success of democracy in India it is not from any external threat, whether from Red China or Pakistan, but from the red tape, bureaucracy and the neglect of intellectuals on the part of politicians in power who prefer office to their party and their party to their country.

Red tape in administration has become more rigid and more complicated than it ever was during the British regime. It is hard to understand why Indian leaders who shook off British imperialism never thought of suiting the administration to the emerging democratic forms of the country. I am convinced that India's bureaucracy is the worst in the world and that the economic and spiritual expense of maintaining the top heavy administrative structure is exhorbitant. Consequently economic planning yields far less than the best results. India must have the largest number of cabinet ministers, deputy ministers, secretaries, deputy secretaries and under secretaries both at the center and in the states than any other country. No other country of the world has such a complicated machinery of government, having wheels within wheels *ad infinitum*. India today needs specialization in industry, science and engineering. Instead she has such a craze for specialization in administration of policies and plans that years are often wasted in the execution of projects because two, three or four departments of government do not see eye to eye in minor details and go on perpetually exchanging notes and comments, which must pass and pass again through channel after channel. The whole system of administration, which was based on doubt and distrust to suit the British, not only continues to exist as it did but has become worse. The impersonal attitude of officials in executing state and national projects often comes to apathy and criminal negligence towards the teeming millions of India with their urgent needs for bare necessities. Unless drastic changes are brought about in India's administrative setup, and unless bureaucrats become intelligent, devoted public servants, the economic development of India will continue to move at a snail's pace. This topheavy expense and wastage in administration are great hindrances to India's economic progress. They obstruct efficiency and smooth working and make development programs mere paper plans. Administration must be attuned to democratic development.

It is unnecessary to provide tedious details of the wastage of Indian talent here, but it is commonly known that the structure of officialdom and white collar employment which India inherited from the British Government aimed to strengthen British imperialism by using Indian talent in routine office and clerical work. As in the past so today engineers and the highly technical officers in India waste much of their time in granting leave to subordinate personnel, in looking into files for transfers and posting of staff, and in sheer make-work and busy-work. I have talked with engineers and technicians in various fields who are disgusted with the jobs entrusted to them and who admit that their specialisation has not been of practical utility to the nation. Obviously what India needs today is a drastic change in governmental organisation and in the attitude of bureaucrats and public officials.

What I have just expressed here has been very recently expressed in another way by the masses of India in the fourth General Elections. It is true that the national and democratic ideology of the ruling party, the Indian National Congress, is probably better than any communal or leftist ideology for the progress of India's democracy and its economic development. But as I try to point out in the last chapter of this book, *man is higher than ideologies,* and if an ideology or institution fails to deliver the goods and is not able to improve the lot of the lower strata of society, it is bound to stand self-condemned. In spite of the great sacrifice of the leaders of the Congress Party in the past, in spite of the fact that this party rendered great service to the Indian nation before and after the attainment of freedom in 1947, the masses in the fourth general elections have shown their dissatisfaction with the Congress regime by defeating the ruling party in at least seven States, and by returning an overwhelming majority of legislators and members of parliament in some of these states from parties other than the Congress Party.

I write these lines more than two years after completing the last chapter of this book. Events have, however, proved the truth of my observations. The prestige of the Congress Party is on the wane, simply because it has not delivered the goods. I do not subscribe to the view that people have been suddenly politically awakened or that the masses can understand the slogans of "Communism", "Socialism" and "Mixed Economy", or that they have more sympathy with leftist or rightist ideologies. The main causes of the defeat of the Congress Party almost everywhere have been that it failed to control prices, it failed to alleviate the food shortage significantly, and it failed to maintain rapport with the masses. Congress leaders turned haughty, conceited and antidemocratic in their attitude towards the masses. All the Food Ministers of the States with one exception were defeated, including the central Food Minister. The opposition parties won more because the people were sick of the long drawn-out Congress regime than because of their positive preference for other parties. If the warnings I mentioned in the last chapter are not heeded, and if the Congress Party continues to be power hungry and adopts questionable means of influencing votes, the next general elections in 1972 will bring about a total disintergration of the foremost democratic organization of India. However this event would not necessarily bring doom to India's democracy or see the dawn of communism in India. I am more certain that it would ultimately lead to the formation of two or three major parties which would be able to maintain a working democracy in this great country. Dictatorship or a military regime or totalitarianism of any kind is ruled out in India for a very long time to come.

Neglect of education has been another cause of the sluggishness of India's economy. However, the emphasis on the improvement of quality at the cost of quality in this field has certainly brought about a general awakening among the students. While I do not approve of the extreme lack of discipline on the part of some students in various states of India, the so-called students' unrest, which is sometimes held to be the result of interference by political parties in the affairs of education, does indicate that democratic tendencies are sure to gain strength in the youth of India. One indication of this is that Mr. Kamaraj, the President of the Congress Party who has thrice brought about a peaceful election of the Prime Minister of India after Nehru (twice unanimously), was defeated in the general elections in the state of Madras (his native state) by the student leader. It is noteworthy that the Congress Party has not been able to return even a single candidate for Parliament from this large state. Whether based on real grievances or otherwise, the demonstrations are sure sign of the political awakening and the assertion of the fundamental rights of the individual in a democracy. An American statesman recently remarked that the United States also had to pass through the pangs of public unrest before becoming a mature democracy. The world is watching the great experiment of democracy in India, especially in the context of the experiment of Maoism in Red China. This small book is intended as a contribution to the understanding of India in the present context of world affairs.

I wish to express my gratitude to those persons who have aided me in the preparation and publication of this book. I am indebted to Dr. Stanley M. Daugert, Chairman of the Philosophy Department, Western Washington State College, Bellingham, Washington, for his editing. I am highly obliged to Dr. D. Mookherjee of the Department of Geography, Western Washington State College, for substantially revising the chapter on economic development. His wife, Mrs. Supriya Mookherjee, was kind enough to help me in preparing the manuscript and I express my thanks to her. I also express my indebtedness to my wife, Mrs. Bhagya Sharma, who originally typed the manuscript. I am grateful to the administration of Western Washington State College, Bellingham, Washington, for providing me facilities to complete this book during my visiting professorship in the summers of 1965 and 1966. Finally, I am grateful to Dr. Victor J. Andrew and Mrs. Andrew, Claremont, California and also to Miss Ruth M. Weil, Long Beach, California, for the exchange of ideas which helped to improve the book.

March, 1967   I. C. SHARMA

Dedication

This book is dedicated to

MR. LYNDON B. JOHNSON,

The President of the United States, as a token of appreciation for his unstinted devotion to the cause of freedom and democracy.

I. C. SHARMA

CHAPTER I

The Question and Its Implications

Why has India not gone Red? This is a serious and vital question both for the man in the street and for the politician in all parts of the world. On its face it is a short, simple question summed up in six words. But in answering it one must recall the historical background of political upheaval in the first half of the 20th century in India and in the whole world, the two world wars, the alliance of the democracies with Soviet Russia, the Chinese Revolution, and, above all, the ideological and technological war between democracy and communism which faces us today. The answer to this deceptively simple question has implications for the future of world politics and hence for the future of mankind.

The question is posed not only on behalf of India as a nation, but on behalf of a way of life, on behalf of the philosophy of democracy and the free world. The emergence of India, after a long subjugation, as the world's largest democratic nation was an event unprecedented in the history of the world. The adoption of democracy by over four hundred million people with two hundred million voters who were until recently considered unfit for any form of self-government (on the grounds of an illiteracy rate of over 80%) is without doubt a unique political experiment in the history of civilization, an experiment without parallel. India's success in conducting the experiment for a decade and a half, especially demonstrated in the successful holding of three general elections, has disproved the theory that literacy is a necessary prerequisite for the adoption of democracy. The achievements of Indian democracy in social, political, and economic areas, and the steady march of this country towards an overall general progress, in spite of the greatest hurdles both national and international, are facts which

1

must be borne in mind by the reader. These facts are usually over-looked or considered trivial, although they are most crucial for India and for the whole world.

It is worth noting that China, the greatest country nearest India, which was known for its ancient culture and philosophy, and which was not faced with as grave problems as India, adopted Commun-ism, but India has remained free. India's attaining freedom was not due to the fact that Communist propaganda was lacking (it wasn't), nor was it due merely to the fact that the effort of the Cominform to spread its ideology in India was forcibly checked by the demo-cratic government of India. It was owing to many other important factors that India could remain free. China's culture, philosophy, religion and political institutions bowed to Communism, but India maintained its cultural and political integrity. A Chinese philos-opher once asked me in a students' gathering in an American college why India, which had given birth to Buddhism, could not retain it, while China had adhered to it throughout. My answer was that India had something better and more sustaining than the nihilistic philosophy of Buddhism, and that the conquest of Communism over Chinese culture was some proof of the truth of my assertion.

The historical background of India is therefore of great import-ance, especially her cultural and philosophical background. The history of India is indicative of the fact that a democratic way of life with freedom of thought and action could alone be an accept-able way of life for the Indians. When Alexander the Great invaded India in the fourth century B. C., he encountered states in the northern territory of India which were democratic. The king in Vedic times was always advised by a ministerial cabinet and an assembly. It is mentioned that two democratic bodies advised the king in political and administrative matters. These bodies were called Sabha, or assembly, and Samiti, or council. The office of the king in the beginning was not hereditary but elective. During the reign of Asoka the Great (third century B. C.) there was com-plete religious freedom, although the king had adopted Buddhism and propagated this religion in foreign countries. Because of reli-gious freedom the great religious reformer, Shankaracharya, could reconvert the whole of India from Buddhism to Hinduism by defeating the Buddhist philosophers in debates in his whirlwind walking tour through the length and breadth of this vast country. This event was one of the most amazing phenomena in human history. Buddha's finest ethics of nonviolence, on whose account India is still regarded as the apostle of peace, was not accepted as a religion by the masses and classes of India because the philosophy on which this religion was based was an absolute nihilism. This philosophy did appeal to China, however, whose tradition had been entirely influenced by the notion of a godless absolute Nature, or Tao, resignation to which was considered the highest virtue. The philosophy of constant change and flux advocated by Buddhism condescends to the revolutionary philosophy of Marxism because it denies the existence of the changeless spirit or God in the midst of evolution and flux. We shall return to this point in the sequel. But in the meantime it is important to note that a skeptical philosophy of life like that of Buddhism is consonant with the acceptance of Communism, which, however, is a poor substitute for a spiritual religion. The lack of conviction in a spiritual order creates a vacuum which is easily filled by the absolutistic and the totalitarian philosophy of Communism which in turn disguises itself as a humanism.

Moverover, hunger and starvation, squalor and poverty are prerequisites to the growth and spread of Communism. When economic deterioration is accompanied by maladministration, injustice and political suppression, Communistic elements are reinforced. India showed all these symptoms of the Communistic fever and yet it did not suffer from the disease when the British ruled. Again her spiritual strength kept her virtually immune from Communism after attaining independence. In the face of poverty, want, hunger and economic depression India could voluntarily have chosen Communism when she attained independence. But she did not, for good and sufficient reasons. Her cultural and religious background, her faith in "unity in diversity" and the success of democratic government and a democratic economy—all are factors jointly responsible for the rejection of Communism on the part of the Indian nation. It is noteworthy that Indian democracy had to undergo unprecedented tests before and after its birth and yet could survive all opposition.

Red China's attack on India, which was generated by the jealousy of the Chinese Communist government towards the successes of Indian democracy, aimed at the dismemberment of the Indian nation with a view to bringing about panic and chaos, the most favorable conditions for the spread of revolutionary Communism.

But unexpectedly for her, Red China's invasion gave a final blow to Communist elements in India and made India even stronger in standing up against further possible onslaughts of violence. I will have to expand upon all these matters in this book to answer the question, Why has India not gone Red?

India's seventy-year nonviolent fight for freedom—which was not bloodless, for hundreds of thousands of Indian patriots lost their lives in it—is another factor which has given spiritual and moral strength to India. Gandhi's creed of non-violence is not the creed of the coward, but of the brave and courageous who are prepared to hazard all but honor for the cause of freedom and justice. The application of this philosophy to life, the sincere belief in non-violence on the part of millions of Indians who divested themselves of their differences of caste, creed, language and province to achieve political independence, trained them to stand against all odds for the unity of the nation and the maintenance of their freedom. The cultural and economic blow given to truncated India by the forced partition of the country, and the fanning of the fires of fanaticism by theocratic and bigotted Muslims of Pakistan could not make the Indian nation give up its secular democracy, and yet fifty million Muslims have continued to live in India as its true citizens, having full representation is state assemblies, parliament, state cabinets, the central ministry, government service and the ambassadorial service. This fact has further strengthened the Indian nation and has proved that a democratic way of life transcends religion and communes of the Red Chinese kind, yet guarantees religious and communal freedom. Such freedoms are thwarted by Communism and theocracy, examples of which are to be found in Red China and Pakistan, respectively. The success of a secular democracy in India is a challenge to the fanaticism of Communistic ideology, which abolishes religious distinctions by physical force. Hence I will explain how the secular democracy of India made headway in spite of all the odds it had to face.

The near civil war conditions created by the exercise of freedom granted to the ruling princes by departing British rulers were the first harsh music to be faced by the infant democracy of India in 1947. No government without integrity and cool self-possession could have attempted much less succeeded in bringing about a bloodless revolution resulting in the merger of about five hundred and sixty princely states with the rest of India. The achievement of such political unity was a herculean task successfully performed by the naive democracy of India. The greatest hurdle to the success of Indian democracy was the prevalence of illiteracy among 90% of its citizens. Education, or at least literacy, had been supposed a pre-requisite for the successful introduction and conduct of democracy. But the granting of an unconditional adult franchise in India and the peaceful conduct of three large general elections have disproved the common sense theory of the precondition of literacy for a democracy. Ignorance and illiteracy are the most favorable conditions for the spread of Communism. But India withstood these handicaps as a democracy, for because of its deep rooted traditions the teeming millions of India are educated, cultured and civilized—though they are illiterate. Hence they cannot easily be duped by Red propaganda. Repelling the ideological attack of Communism is perhaps more important and more difficult than repulsing its military aggression. The balance of power maintained by stockpiling nuclear weapons is no doubt a successful check against the advancement of Communism in the free world, but the maintenance of the ideological balance of power through the success of democracy is far more important. The successful experiment of democracy among the millions of illiterates in India is a great ideological victory over Communism. I have also therefore to throw light on this aspect of Indian democracy.

The economic progress made by India after her independence is another unprecedented event in her history. India's over six hundred thousand villages, inhabited by over eighty per cent of her population previously dependent on the chance mercy of the monsoon for its agriculture, have adopted new methods of exploiting the soil to increase production and to strike at the roots of hunger and poverty. Huge irrigation projects and hydroelectric schemes are changing the face of India gradually but perceptibly. The change-over from a police state to a democratic state is not an easy task. Old habits die hard. But the zeal and fervor shown by the illiterate villagers in India in furthering community development projects certainly proves that these habits can be substituted by good new ones. This unexpected tendency of adjustment on the part of the average Indian villager has made a real and lasting contribution to the democratic development of the country and has therefore further undermined the chances of Communism. Hence an account of the Indian democracy's political and economic progress is included in this book.

The other important factor which has strengthened India as a democracy, allusion to which has already been made, is the armed attack of Red China on India. This aggression, though calamitous and disastrous for thousands of Indian soldiers who laid down their lives for Indian democracy, has proved to be a blessing in disguise. It has reunited India, saving it from bickering on the minor problems of language and provincialism, and it has exposed the Communist pretenders, thereby bringing political death to Communism. The disillusionment experienced by the politicians and the disenchantment of the common people of India in the face of the hypocrisy of Red China have caused a genuine skepticism in India. At the same time it has resulted in the affirmation of India's faith in democratic western nations. A new confidence generated out of goodwill for America and Britain has spread among the millions of Indian citizens. A brief account of the Red China's aggression is therefore given in the sequel.

If Red Chinese aggression has reaffirmed the unity of India and made it aware of the external danger to its democracy, the behavior of India's religiously fanatic neighbor, Pakistan, has also contributed in its own way to that unity. Many people forget that India fought for freedom for over sixty years through the well-organized Indian National Congress, which was a purely secular party and which always aimed at the establishment of a secular democracy in united India. But, unfortunately, British politicians while ruling India followed the policy of "divide and rule." They sowed seeds of hatred and discord among Indians to strengthen the roots of British imperialism, and, at the time of departing India, they gave her a parting kick by creating a theocratic state of Pakistan out of India. The nationalist politicians who were forced to accept the necessary evil of partition, however, continued to maintain the secular status of India. The presence of over fifty million Muslims in India and their equal status in Indian government as cabinet ministers, members of Parliament, state ministers, ambassadors and governors is also proof of the success of Indian democracy as a secular state. The state of Pakistan, indulging in hatred, bigotry, and religious fanaticism, has been attempting to revive communal hatred in India by false propaganda and by misrepresenting the Kashmir issue, virtually adopting Nazi tactics by claiming itself the champion of all Muslims outside Pakistan. In spite of the great setback caused by the partition India proved that a united India could have made more rapid progress than truncated India. Nevertheless, India would like to see Pakistan flourish as a democracy so that her neighboring state might help the cause of freedom. However, this intention of India has not been recognized or countenanced, and the slogan, "Islam in danger," has remained the keynote of the theocratic politicians of Pakistan. This attitude of India's immediate neighbor, which cannot dissociate itself from India culturally and geographically, is responsible for a greater vigilance on the part of Indian politicians to strengthen the secular character of Indian democracy and to bring about national unity. The whole Kashmir issue is to be studied from this point of view with reference to the facts. A realistic analysis of the Kashmir issue therefore is necessary in this context, and this issue is dispassionately discussed in this book.

Not only problems but persons have also conspicuously influenced the evolution of Indian democracy. Two personalities of contemporary India have particularly nourished Indian nationalism with their self-devotion and self-sacrifice. Gandhi laid down his life for the cause of the unity of India, and Nehru, who was Gandhi's successor as a political philosopher, statesman and nation-builder was first and last a democrat. The outside world is not really aware of the yeoman service rendered by this self-denying great patriot to his nation from his early youth to his recent death. Nehru was totally engrossed in the welfare of India as its prime minister, not because he wished to remain an unrivaled leader, but because he lived only for India. Every day, every hour and every moment of his life was dedicated to the cause of the development of the Indian nation and sustaining the Indian democracy. The sincerity of this realistic idealist was misunderstood and sometimes misused not only by outsiders but even by his own countrymen. His honesty was sometimes a handicap, his straight-forwardness a hindrance, and his liberalism an opening for those who exploited him. But his insight, or, rather, his intuition, has helped the Indian nation to follow the right path and to protect its hard-earned freedom from Communism. It is therefore necessary to throw light on the contribution of Nehru towards strengthening Indian democracy and safeguarding it from internal and external dangers.

Not only have India's challenges and idealogues helped her to maintain democracy, but her policy, particularly the policy of non-alignment, has made a positive contribution to the process of nation building. There are many misunderstandings with regard to the noncommittal attitude of India so far as military alliances with either powerblock are concerned. But misgivings vanish when we compare this policy of the infant Indian democracy with the historically neutral policy of the United States in relation to Europe, a policy held by the United States for a very long time, indeed from its beginning until rather recently. Just as the United States, following Washington's precepts, did not wish to commit herself to any foreign country in Europe, and just as she followed the policy of remaining aloof from the hot politics of Europe, just so has India followed the example of the United States in pursuing an independent course. The policy of not aligning with any nation east or west is giving India breathing space to progress without interference. Moreover, culturally and philosophically India's love for peace and nonviolence urges her diplomats to contribute to peace and not to add fuel to the fire of cold war. For these reasons India has not entered into any military alliance either with West or with Russia or China. It is true that India is a democracy and that the Communist bloc cannot think well of her or wish her well. Red Chinese hypocrisy with regard to the Panch Shila treaty, whose aim was co-existence, and the sudden Chinese attack on India are events which prove the treacherous nature of Communist tactics. One of the aims of Red China was to bring down the prestige of India among the non-aligned nations and to corner India to the point of forcing her to join the Western bloc. The withdrawal of India from the neutral nations, of which India is still the acknowledged leader, would not only degrade India but would also precipitate the overthrow of the smaller Asian nations by the Red Chinese. In view of these facts India's non-alignment policy not only serves her own interests, but it also serves the best interests of the free world. This aspect of the foreign policy of India has immeasurable importance in strengthening the democracy of this great nation and contributing to world peace, and hence it requires a detailed discussion in this book. Our discussion of this policy leads us to the conclusion that for economic, ethical and political reasons India's non-alignment policy is the best policy today.

The most influential factor safeguarding the democratic way of life in India is her strong cultural background which has always inspired faith and confidence among her people, thereby foiling all efforts to woo India to Chinese Communism, the creed of an intellectually starved, spiritually suppressed, famished and frustrated people. It is the last resort of a vacant mind. A loss of conviction in human freedom and an extreme cynicism and pessimism which wring out the soul of man are contributory causes in adopting a totalitarian philosophy like Mao Tse Tung's. Chinese Communism, based on the philosophy of dialectical materialism, is completely negativistic, and in practice means a violent extinction of all parties and the capture of power by totalitarians who rule supreme by resorting to brain-washing and concentration camps, merciless massacre of innocent people, and mass regimentation. All this is diametrically opposed to the ideals and convictions of Indian culture and philosophy. Indians are temperamentally and culturally opposed to any form of political, social, or philosophical ideology or institution which is non-spiritual and nihilistic. Indians may be illiterates but they are not uneducated, as we have already remarked, for they actually live their culture and philosophy, their ethics and religion. Nothing is dearer to an Indian than his faith and spiritual conviction. He firmly believes that "man eats to live" and that he "does not live to eat." Rightly or wrongly, this view of life is universally accepted in India; hence its cultural background, its catholicism and its faith in individual freedom and the dignity of man are factors which form a steel shield against the philosophy of the iron curtain. I have therefore devoted a chapter to an exposition of the ideological and cultural background of India, which provides and has always provided an atmosphere most congenial to a democratic way of life.

Having given a systematic account of the above-mentioned factors responsible for India's adherence to democracy as opposed to Communism, I have attempted to make some further observations. In the absence of knowledge of the facts we are bound to misunderstand; misunderstanding leads to an unintelligent and uncalled-for denunciation of each other, and denunciation leads again to misunderstanding, thereby creating a vicious circle. But luckily the Western world is conscious of this contingency and America, particularly, is anxious to understand India. The same is true of India, which is anxious to learn more about science, technology and the democratic way of life from America. There are many similarities between these two great nations. India like America is a country inhabited by many nationalities and races. It represents a unity in diversity like the United States. Its problems are not greatly different from America's. Both nations are opposed to totalitarianism. India is the oldest nation and the youngest democracy, whereas America is the youngest nation, but the oldest democracy. If India is the land of spirituality and saints, America is the country of the pilgrims who hazarded all for religious freedom. Mutual understanding and cooperation of the two can redeem oppressed humanity from the fear of domination by totalitarianism. The struggle between freedom and totalitarianism, between democracy and dictatorship and between capitalism and Communism is not merely technological, but is also ideological. The success of India as the largest democracy in the world would be a crushing ideological defeat to Communism. China and India are the two great political experiments in Communism and democracy respectively. The adoption of Communism on the part of China is mainly due to its cultural background, which is just the opposite of India's cultural background. A comparison of these two cultures would reveal how the other uncommitted nations can be saved from falling victim to the dangerous experiment of totalitarianism. India's social, political and economic progress would certainly be a source of inspiration to other underdeveloped countries. But caution and care are necessary on the part of the sponsors of democracy and freedom. In the last chapter of this book I try to point out what can be done to foster freedom and democracy and to save human civilization from the horror of a nuclear destruction, which without great caution might become a reality. We should not forget that man is higher than ideologies.

A survey of the economic, political and cultural aspect of Indian democracy reveals that its success depends on various factors. However, the most important factor for the preservation of democracy in India is her realistic attitude towards the western democracies in general and toward the United States in particular. Until recently the United States has not intimidated India to force her to give up her non-alignment policy, and until recently her economic aid to all underdeveloped countries transcended ideological considerations. Nevertheless a number of misunderstandings due to lack of knowledge about the United States and her people is responsible for much of the misinformation of Indian politicians and their mistaken attitudes and actions towards the United States. Hence in the concluding chapter I have attempted to throw light on this aspect of Indian democracy and to make suggestions to avoid political errors.

CHAPTER II

The Labor Pains of
Indian Democracy

Like the pre-independent United States before 1776, India until 1947 was governed by the British crown and the British parliament thousands of miles away. Like the American colonies which became the United States, India had no representation. Like those same colonies India had to fight for her independence, though non-violently, for about seventy years as compared with the seven-years' war of American independence. Whereas America adopted the slogan, "No taxation without representation," Indians raised the slogan, "Freedom is our birthright." Coincidently, another important affinity exists between India and America so far as India's attainment of freedom is concerned. The freedom movement in India was throughout undertaken by a national organization known as the Indian National Congress, a body which had representation from all the communities and provinces of India. It is noteworthy that this political body, now the leading political party in Indian democracy, was founded in 1885 in India by an American missionary, Mr. A. O. Hume. This American will ever be remembered as the pioneer of Indian independence in the political history of India.

India and America had two great leaders who dedicated their lives to the causes of national unity and equality, men who were perhaps ahead of their time. I am hinting at the parallels between the lives of Abraham Lincoln and Mahatma Gandhi, both of whom achieved their national missions and both of whom were assassinated soon after their success. Both were great leaders who adopted the profession of law and both were the men of the masses. In spite of these similarities, however, the political history of India is quite

different from that of America. The Indian struggle for independence had a checkered career and had to pass through various
stages over a longer period. Although the Indians did not take
arms against the government and declare open war, yet the non-
violent struggle made the British more furious and vindictive than
perhaps the American revolt had made them.

The struggle was non-violent, the method was "satyagraha," or
"truthful protest," and the attitude adopted was to hate the evil but
not the evil-doer—to kill caesarism but not to murder Caesar.

Prior to the attainment of independence, the entire administration of the country, except for the internal government of the
princely states, was in the hands of the bureaucrats representing the
British crown. Even in the princely states where the personal will—
or rather the whim—of the ruler was law, the British resident was
the supreme power. He was not only the supreme observer, but also
the chief advisor of the ruler in matters of policy. Hence, in spite
of the princes' monarchical powers, their behavior was not free except in their private life, which was mostly a life of indulgence.
Most of these rulers ruthlessly suppressed the freedom movement
in their states to please the British government which, in turn,
in cynical *quid pro quo* fashion, conferred titles on these rulers. The
higher their title, the greater their loyalty to the British crown.
Furthermore the rulers appointed a number of sub-rulers, or feudal
lords, who ruthlessly exploited the peasants and laborers, and they
also had a number of permanent servants who were virtually slaves
for they served the family of their feudal lords generation after generation. When the daughter of a feudal lord married the son of another feudal lord, a few servants, male and female, would also be
offered as a dowry accompanying the bride. These feudal lords always flattered the ruler and received titles and gifts from him as the
mark of their loyalty, as the ruler received similar titles from the
British crown. The British government fostered this system because
it strengthened the roots of British imperialism—at the cost of the
freedom of tens of millions of the subjects of those states who were
made to believe that their ruler had divine rights and that they
should always obey his orders blindly. This suppression and humiliation was no less than that experienced by the French before their
Revolution or by the Russians before theirs of 1917.

The children of these feudal lords went to special schools and
most of the sons of the rulers were sent to England for their educa-

tion. The purpose of providing such education was to make the princes dedicated to the British life, to learn to speak English fluently, to see and learn the "glories" of England, and to be more loyal to the British queen or king, the Empress or Emperor of India. These objectives were almost perfectly achieved, and when these English-educated princes ascended their throne in their respective states they ruthlessly suppressed the freedom movement, sent the national leaders to jail, where they were often tortured, and confiscated their property.

I emphasize this aspect of these Indian princes' English education because many people in the west mistakenly think that the British educated the Indians in democracy. Many false notions about Indians were let loose by her erstwhile British masters who wanted to impress upon the world, particularly upon the freedom-loving western democracies, that everything Indian was uncouth, heathen, anti-social, anti-ethical and barbaric. It was in the interest of British imperialism not to allow the Western world to know the rich culture and philosophy of India, and to distort the facts in such a manner as to justify their occupation of India. Within India the British maneuvered to suppress the people by fostering feudalism in the princely states and by creating rifts between Hindus and Muslims in British India. Outside India, they cleverly propagated the notion that Indians were barbarians and that they were unworthy of any kind of self-government. How Indian culture and Indian social structure were well-suited to the adoption of democracy I will discuss later. But I want to bring this fact to the notice of the reader, that the British rulers never really wished Indians educated to adopt democracy or to improve economically, industrially and scientifically. The aim of introducing English education in India was merely to procure clerks and typists to run the British administration smoothly. The princely rulers were educated in England to learn loyalty to the British throne. Besides the princes, the sons of wealthy industrialists and high officials, who received very large salaries and titles for their fidelity and loyalty to the British crown, also went to England for their so-called "higher education." The rest of India was kept in the blessed darkness of ignorance. Hardly ten per cent of the Indians were literate when the British left in 1947. How can we possibly assume then that the British had any idea of training Indians for self-goverment? On the contrary, they corrupted the higher class Indians by training them in loyalty to the British crown and they received the benefits of that loyalty. This aspect of British policy is too often and too easily forgotten, and hence the labor pains that the Indian democracy had to experience before its birth are overlooked.

An atmosphere of illiteracy was naturally more congenial for British imperialism. British bureaucrats not only made few efforts to educate the Indians but also at the same time they were constantly conscious of their being the rulers. They disliked, even hated the Indian people, the Indian language and Indian culture. They were under the impression that the millions of illiterates could never become politically conscious. The dreams of the British were seen to be unfounded when Ghandhi gave a clarion call, and when these teeming millions resorted to the method of satyagraha, or non-violent protest of truth. The truth was that the British were following a dual policy of fostering "equality, liberty and fraternity" in Britain and of keeping millions of Indians as their slaves, thereby fostering imperialism outside Britain. But satyagraha gained ground and shook the foundation of the British Empire in a few decades. Many obstacles had to be overcome before it could succeed. Two obstacles were poverty and the British-engineered and British-fostered differences between the Hindus and the Muslims, the two major communities of India. I want to discuss these two handicaps in the way of Indian freedom, and then proceed to describe the birth of Indian democracy.

As already stated, the overwhelming majority of Indians were illiterate and hence quite ignorant of the fact that they were slaves. The subjects of the princely states were in fact slaves of slaves, because their rulers were proud of their loyalty to the British king. In British India a Deputy Commissioner, invariably a Britisher, ruled supreme over his district and was the uncrowned king of the area under his jurisdiction. He was the district magistrate, the district administrator, the district collector of revenue, and the highest executive officer of the district all in one. He represented the British crown and was honored like a king. He lived in palatial quarters guarded by the police and held a daily court attended by the leading citizens, businessmen and landlords of the area who considered it an honor to be favored with a five-minute interview. They were only a chosen few, the favorites of the British commissioner, and were the trusted informants of the British government. They received gifts of land and other favors for their loyalty. The majority, illiterate and unaware of their right to freedom, respected these flatterers of the British government, taking them to be demigods. The honored agents of the British who helped their administration were sometimes created honorary magistrates and were also favored with titles, which added new feathers to their caps every year. The poor laborers and farmers were like dumbdriven cattle and were over-awed by these agents of the British government. No one could get into government service unless he belonged to the charmed circle or unless he was related to one of these highly respectable flatterers. Thus a heirarchy of pro-British officers, government servants and informants became an efficient machinery to run the British administration without any opposition whatsoever from the ignorant millions, who remained calm and passive subjects of the British crown. The deputy commissioner was responsible to the divisional commissioner, the commissioner was subordinate to the governor of the province, the governor was responsible to the viceroy and the governor-general of India, who was under the secretary of state in the British homeland. The secretary of state, who might not even have seen India, ruled the great country on behalf of His or Her Majesty, the King or Queen of England and Emperor or Empress of India.

This heirarchy of imperialistic administration with a top-heavy bureaucratic government machinery was run by the Indian civil service, the incumbents of which were selected in Britain only. The laborer and the farmer worked from morning until night in the sweltering heat and the freezing cold without being able to get two square meals a day, whereas the British bureaucrats, who received fabulous salaries and literally had almost all the comforts available on earth, exported Indian wealth to England. In India these so-called "civil servants" lived like demigods and often did not descend to earth, for they had the best possible means of communication while moving on Indian soil. Carriages driven by half a dozen horses in pre-automobile days, and, later on, all sorts of the very latest models of motor cars were at their disposal at the cost of the Indian exchequer. When they appeared in public meetings and had to walk to the stage from their comfortable cars, they walked on soft velvet which was especially purchased for this purpose at public expense. The costliest furniture, cushions, carpets and every piece of crockery for their kitchen was purchased from England, again at the cost of the Indian exchequer. A British bureaucrat in India had scores of servants engaged by the government and hence made practically no effort because a servant was always there to serve the Sahib (literally, "master"). A waterman was necessary for quenching the thirst of the Sahib, a Sawar (cyclist) was there for running errands, a peon for lifting his files, a bearer for waiting at the door of his office, a watchman for night duty, a policeman at the gate of his palatial bungalow, a gardener for his domestic garden, a butler for his kitchen, and so on and on. These are facts not generally known to Westerners, who were given to believe that the Britishers were simply training illiterate Indians to adopt democracy, and that their bonafides as guides and sponsors of Indian democracy could not be doubted. The fact remains that the great wealth of India was literally exported to Britain, and the teeming millions lived in poverty, want, hunger, illiteracy and ignorance. It was a herculean task to bring about a political awakening amongst these people and to make them conscious of their birthright of independence and self-government. Gandhi was the first leader who proved equal to the task. He identified himself with laborers and farmers, he dressed like them and spoke to them in their own language. He mobilized the masses and trained them to fight the non-violent battle, first to win political independence and then to work for the prosperity of the nation. But the task was very tedious and dangerous, full of obstacles, oppositions and hardships. Gandhi trained his countrymen to face all these odds and to prepare to sacrifice everything but honor to win the non-violent war of Indian independence.

It was natural for the British government and the British diplomats to put all possible obstacles in the way of Gandhi's efforts to awaken his countrymen. The Empire, with its great material benefits, was much dearer to them than the sense of justice and equality. I will refer to acts of violence and mass-killing by the British government in the sequel. It will suffice here to say that the British administration in India adopted all means, fair and foul, to suppress the freedom movement, to send the leaders to jails, to confiscate their property, and to create a rift among the two major communities of India, Hindus and Muslims.

As a matter of fact, Hindus and Muslims are not two nationalities, but merely two of the many communities of India. The difference between them is only a difference of religion, and not of race, language or culture. They have been living together for thousands of years, have been nourished like two flowers in the same soil. Even when Akbar the Great, the Moghul Emperor, was ruling India, there was harmony and peace between the Hindus, the Muslims, the Jainas and the Buddhists. Is it not surprising that out of the various religious communities—Christians, Jainas, Parsis, Sikhs, Buddhists and Muslims—only the last was singled out by the British to be the most deserving of an independent state, Pakistan? But this surprise will vanish when the reader realizes that the root cause of the physical partition of India was not the diversity of religions, but the diplomacy of the British government. I will return to this point when I deal with the partition of India. But I would like to refer here to the subversive aspect of the British policy of "divide and rule," which was the cornerstone of British diplomacy in India.

The British have followed the foreign policy of balancing power in Europe for centuries. But this policy was converted into the policy of "divide and rule" in India. It was in the eighteenth century that the East India Company began the military conquest of India. It was successful in doing so because by playing one territorial ruler against the other it was able to divide the princes and yet retain control. But in 1857 the Hindus and the Muslims united and revolted against the East India Company. After the suppression of this first attempt to shake off British rule, the administration of India was transferred to the British parliament by the East India Company. Twenty-eight years after this unsuccessful armed revolt there was founded the Indian National Congress, which had representatives from all the communities and religions of India, and which ultimately undertook the non-violent struggle for Indian independence. Hindus and Christians, Parsis and Muslims, Jainas and Sikhs—all formed this organization and all offered non-violent resistance, a mass movement of satyagraha, to the British rule in India. To counteract this united effort of the Indians, the British government again resorted to the policy of "divide and rule." When political reforms were introduced as a result of the freedom movement, separate electorates for Hindus and Muslims were created as the basis of such reforms; then when local self-government was introduced, the electorate was divided into Muslims and non-Muslims. Moreover, when the British diplomats saw that in spite of their efforts to bring about disunity between Hindus and Muslims these two communities (along with others) combined to offer non-violent resistance, they began subversive activities to generate communal riots. These riots were undoubtedly engineered in the beginning by British administrators, who were responsible for law and order in the whole country. The tactics used in such riots were to create mischief at the festivals of the Muslims or the Hindus.

In spite of these handicaps India was able to unite in her struggle for independence due to the unique leadership of Mahatma Gandhi, who trained the masses of India to win freedom by the force of love and non-violence. It is necessary to refer briefly to the technique of non-violence here. This method of love, as opposed to that of war, took a long time to succeed and involved much sacrifice of life and limb. But it should not be forgotten that it did attain unique success and had far-reaching salutary results insofar as India's relations with the western democracies and with Britain in particular are concerned. Had India adopted violence, had she retaliated when thousands of her people were killed by the use of force by the British, her relations with Britain after the attainment of independence would have not only been strained but perhaps severed. She would probably not have remained a part of the Commonwealth. Gandhi always advocated love and friendship for the British. Even when atrocities and mass-killing were practiced by British officers and when other Congress leaders became furious, Gandhi remained cool and composed, and successfully convinced his colleagues to return love for hatred and virtue for vice.

From the moment Gandhi appeared on the political scene of India, he urged his countrymen not to follow violence while demanding freedom from the British. During World War I when other leaders of the Congress believed that it was the best opportunity for India to force the British government to set India free, Gandhi did not approve. Rather he suggested that at such a critical juncture Indians should help save the British empire. He hoped that good sense would prevail among the British to make India independent after the war, if India co-operated with Britain at the time of that catastrophe. With this hope he advocated co-operation with the British government in the war effort. His hope was generated by the announcement of the new British policy towards India in the parliament on the twentieth of August, 1917. This announcement promised dominion status to India. Commenting on this announcement, Louis Fischer says that it envisaged not only the increasing association of Indians in every branch of administration, but also the granting of "self-governing institutions with a view to the progressive realization of responsible government in India as an integral part of the British empire."

Indians followed the lead of Gandhi, and thousands of persons who were recruited for the army fought bravely in the war and helped bring about the British and Allied victory. But when the war was over, all the hopes of the Indians ended in smoke. Instead of getting dominion status, they were deprived even of their civil liberties, which would normally have been restored to the Indians after the war. Commenting upon this bewilderment of the Indians, Louis Fischer has remarked, "When World War I ended in November, 1918, Indians expected a restoration of the considerable civil liberties they enjoyed under British rule in normal times. They were painfully surprised when the war-time rigors were continued under the Rowlatt Acts, passed by the New Delhi Imperial Legislative Council on March 18, 1919."

The natural reaction of the Indian leaders and masses was to express their resentment toward this attitude of the British government. Gandhi gave the clarion call for satyagraha, which was to take the shape of violating some minor law to court arrest. Gandhi, while commending the satyagraha pledge signed by six hundred persons in Bombay, remarked, "The pledge is an attempt to introduce the religious spirit into politics. We may no longer believe in the doctrine of tit for tat, we may not meet hatred with hatred, violence with violence, evil with evil . . . Return good for evil." But prior to starting the satyagraha, the country observed a general strike. On the whole the strike was successful, but in some places where police threatened and even attacked the crowds, the untrained masses did indulge in violence. Gandhi himself was dissatisfied with the behavior of his own countrymen. He admitted his own error and called off the satyagraha immediately. In one important city of the state of Punjab, Amritsar, the excesses of the administration were accompanied by the banishment of two prominent leaders of the Congress Party, Suiffuddin Kitchlu, a Muslim, and Dr. Satyapal, a Hindu.

The resentment of the public toward the maltreatment of these leaders indicated the unity of the Hindus and the Muslims. In this city about twenty thousand unarmed people had gathered to hold a meeting in a garden, called Jallianwala Bagh. There was only one entrance to the garden, which was surrounded by houses. While the meeting was being peacefully held, a British army officer,

Brigadier General Dyer, entered the scene with armed soldiers and opened fire on the peaceful crowd without warning. Innocent men, women and children were mercilessly massacred in this ruthless shooting. When an inquiry was made by a committee appointed by the British government, this heinous crime of General Dyer was dismissed as "a mistaken conception of his duty," and no action was taken against him. General Dyer wrote in his official dispatch: "It was no longer a question of merely dispersing the crowd, but one of producing a sufficient moral effect not only on those who were present, but more especially throughout Punjab. There would be no question of undue severity." When the action of such a hard-hearted officer was approved by exonerating him, it was natural for the Indian leaders and patriots to take action. In the same year, however, the British parliament announced the Montague Chelmsford reforms, according to which a partial administration was to be handed over the elected ministers in the provinces. When the annual convention of the Indian National Congress was held near the Jallianwala Bagh, where the merciless massacre had taken place a few months earlier, the Congress leaders advocated direct action and complete non-cooperation with the British government. Some leaders made fiery speeches and called for the rejection of the Chelmsford reforms. But Gandhi, the votary of love and non-violence, calmed all of them and succeeded in convincing the convention that hatred should be returned by love. Ever since, love for the British has never been repudiated by India. This is the reason India never severed its connection with Britain, and why she forgot all the wounds inflicted by the British during the struggle for independence. This attitude of love towards hostile rulers was not mere idealism. It ultimately had a profound effect, and raised the morale of India. India was consistent in her behavior when she chose to remain in the Commonwealth after independence. This consistency has helped her to maintain independence and to remain in closer touch with the western democracies. It was due to this very policy that India received timely help from Britain when Red China attacked her in 1962. Had Gandhi's advice in the annual convention of 1919 in Amritsar not been heeded, had India adopted an attitude of hatred towards the British before and after independence, perhaps India's foreign policy would have taken a wrong turn.

India has remained unaffected by the Communist ideology because Communism believes in violence and India shuns violence. The adoption of a non-violent method of winning independence shows the non-acceptance of violent Communism on the part of India. Non-violence is not merely a negative attitude, it is a positive approach which aims at changing the heart of the adversary. It requires great moral courage to adopt it. Fearlessness of death is necessary. To call it "passive resistance" is to misunderstand it. Gandhi believed that a great deal of training was necessary for adopting non-violence. He suspended satyagraha whenever he felt that the masses had not yet acquired the undaunted courage to suffer the consequences of non-violent struggle. But he did succeed in infusing the spirt of self-sacrifice among his followers and conducted satyagraha successfully. The success of the satyagraha did involve violence on the part of the British government, however. It would be wrong to say that the non-violent struggle for independence was bloodless. On the contrary, the greater the violence adopted by the British, the more confident the Indians became in the success of non-violence.

Let me cite one example of the successful conduct of this non-violent revolt to support the above remark. In 1930 Gandhi recommended the satyagraha, but this time the masses were very particular in observing discipline. They knew that if they resorted to violence of any kind, Gandhi would call off the satyagraha. This mass civil disobedience, which aimed at breaking the salt law, was begun by Gandhi's twenty-four days' march to Dandi, a sea coast town, where he had decided to initiate the movement, the aim of which was to urge the British government to lift the ban on preparing salt out of sea water freely. No one could prepare salt out of sea water or even pick up salt from the beaches. The only legal way to obtain salt was to purchase it from the government salt monopoly. Gandhi argued that salt law was unjust, because poor men in India, who used salt more than the rich, were heavily taxed for a blessing of nature. When Gandhi marched towards Dandi thousands of Indians followed him. Gandhi was sent to jail as a criminal for breaking the salt law. All over the country the law was violated and thousands of people were jailed. During this non-violent mass movement twenty-five hundred volunteers under the guidance of the well-known poetess, Congress leader Mrs. Sarojini Naidu, and Manilal Gandhi offered satyagraha by marching towards the prohibited area of the Dharsana Salt Works, one hundred and fifty miles from Bombay. These volunteers were instructed not even to raise their hand if attacked by the police. They provided a supreme example of courage and self-sacrifice while marching towards the prohibited area to break the law. I would like to quote here a passage from Louis Fischer's book on Gandhi to bring home the spirit of non-violence to the reader. Fischer writes, "Webb Miller, the well-known correspondent of the United Press, who died in England during the second World War, was on the scene and described the event first in dispatches and then in his book . . . Manilal Gandhi, second son of the Mahatma, advanced at the head of the marchers and approached the great salt pans which were surrounded by ditches and barbed wire and guarded by four hundred Surat policemen under the command of six British officers." "In complete silence," Miller writes, "The Gandhi men drew up and halted a hundred yards from the stockade. The officers ordered them to return but they continued to step forward. Suddenly at a word of command . . . policemen rushed upon the advancing marchers and rained blows on their heads with their steel-shod lathis (staves). Not one of the marchers even raised an arm to fend off the blows. They went down like tenpins. I heard the sickening wack of the blades on unprotected skulls. The waiting crowd of marchers groaned and sucked in their breath in sympathetic pain at every blow. Those struck down fell sprawling, unconscious or writhing with fractured skulls or broken shoulders. . . . The survivors, without breaking ranks, silently and doggedly marched on until struck down. When the first column was laid low, another advanced." "Although everyone knew," Webb Miller writes, "that within a few minutes he would be beaten down, perhaps killed, I could detect no sign of wavering or fear. They marched steadily, with heads up, without the encouragement of music or cheering or any possibility that they might escape injury or death. The police rushed out and methodically and mechanically beat down the second column. There was no fight, no struggle, the marchers simply walked forward until struck down. Another group of twenty-five advanced and sat down." "The police," Miller testifies, "commenced savagely kicking the seated men in the abdomen and testicles. Another column presented itself. Enraged, the police dragged them by their arms and feet and threw them into the ditches." "One was dragged to a ditch where I stood," Miller recorded, "the splash of his body doused me with muddy water. Another policeman dragged a Gandhi man to the ditch, threw him in, and belabored him over the head with his lathi. Hour after hour stretcher bearers carried back a stream of inert, bleeding men."

I have cited this passage to give the reader an idea of how the votaries of non-violence and truth suffered tortures and death inflicted upon them by the British rulers. This is just one incident, which was reported by a press representative. But hundreds of such incidents involving the sacrifice of thousands of unknown soldiers of the war of independence occurred in the length and breadth of India. These incidents were not truly reported even within India. The world has seen the emergence of India as a free nation in 1947, but the injustices, tyrannies and tortures to which millions of innocent and non-violent Indians were subjected are not known to the world. The memories of their sufferings are yet fresh in the minds of the present generation and hence the hard-earned freedom is dearer to millions of Indians than their lives. The united reaction of the Indian nation towards the Communist attack in 1962 was therefore quite natural and in keeping with the spirit of self-sacrifice on the part of the Indian people.

India became a democracy not because the British really wanted to see her attain sovereign democratic status gradually, as has wrongly been reported and propagated in the West. The constant use of violence, suppression and repression on the part of the British rulers until 1945 is indicative of the intention of the British to keep India subservient as long as they could. I mention these facts not as a matter of complaint, but to give the reader the historical and factual background of Indian democracy. To say that India has learned a democratic way of life only from the British imperialists is not only to falsify the facts, but also to overlook the democratic potentiality and the patriotism of the Indian people. As long as the British ruled India, they made all possible efforts to crush the spirit of freedom and nationalism. Millions of people suffered when hundreds of thousands of able-bodied Indians were thrown into jails. When the wage earners of the millions of poor families were imprisoned, the illiterate women and innocent children had actually to starve and even to die of starvation. Wearing the national dress in government institutions was a crime. Anyone who put on a Gandhi cap (a white cap made of hand-woven cloth) was taken to be a rebel.

But Gandhi taught us to bear all these hardships and to continue to follow the path of love and non-violence. Ironically enough, when all our national leaders were in jail during World War II, the Communists had full freedom to propagate their ideology, because at that time they were the messengers to Russia, who was an ally of Britain. Under the pretext of propagating allegiance to the Allies among the villagers, these favored Communists tried to preach their violent revolutionary ideology. Prior to the free rein given to the Communists during World War II, practically no one in the villages had heard about Communism. But when all the Congress leaders were in jails, and the masses had no one to guide them, the fifth columnists of Communism, who could now come into the open, preached Marxism freely. This was the greatest disservice done to democracy by the repressive policy of the British government towards the Congress leaders. This was a setback to Indian nationalism, a setback to democracy, and a setback to the free world. The labor pains before the birth of the Indian democracy were therefore not ordinary, but most severe and complicated. But these very pains are also responsible for making India stronger and united against the Red menace today. Whether India can maintain her unique democracy will become clear as we proceed. But we must devote at least one more chapter to the historical background of Indian democracy, for without the thorough knowledge of such background we will not be able to judge intelligently how weak or how strong Indian democracy is. I will therefore undertake a dispassionate survey of the birth of Indian democracy in the next chapter.

CHAPTER III

The Birth of Indian Democracy

I have already mentioned that the struggle for independence in India took a long time. I have also referred to the mass movement of civil disobedience, or satyagraha, led by Gandhi in 1930. It is noteworthy that the non-violent campaign had a lasting effect on the mind of thoughtful British diplomats. A small group of British politicians did favor the gradual emancipation of India, yet they had little influence. On the other hand, the adoption of a high-handed policy by the British bureaucrats and the violation of their promises made the Indians skeptical. Jawaharlal Nehru and Sub-hash Chandra Bose, youthful Congress Party leaders, advocated complete independence instead of dominion status. On January 26, 1930, Nehru, who had been elected the youngest president of the All India Congress at its annual convention, proclaimed complete independence and unfurled the tricolor flag of independence. This was a moral challenge to the British government. Just after this declaration there occurred a sudden surge of political consciousness over the whole of India. The violation of the salt tax law was nationwide, and all Congress Party leaders were thrown into jail. Large-scale strikes and mass demonstrations of protest against British rule all over the country followed.

Under the pressure of national upheaval and commotion, the British government was compelled to call two round-table confer-ences in London, the second of which was attended by Mahatma Gandhi as representative of the Congress Party. However, in the meetings of this conference the British followed the same old policy of trying to create rifts wherever possible. Muslim fanatics like Mr. Jinnah and his group were given importance by the recognition given to the Muslim League as a political body. In spite of the fact that the Congress Party represented all the communities, Hindus, Muslims, Christians, Parsees and Sikhs, etc., British politicians insisted on giving weight to the Muslim League, which was certainly not the representative organization of all the Muslims. Their purpose was quite clear, i.e., to create dissensions and rifts, to divide and rule. The Congress Party could see through the game, however, and as a result the national leaders were not satisfied with the deliberations of the second round-table conference.

It is worth mentioning here that Mr. Jinnah, who later became the sole creator of Pakistan, and the first governor-general of his theocratic state, was not a communalist in the beginning and originally had no idea of a separate state for his group. Until the 1920's he was a staunch supporter of the Congress Party and had full faith in its ideology. In 1917, when Jinnah was a nationalist, he preached co-operation and unity between Hindus and Muslims and pleaded that Muslims not be apprehensive of the domination of the Hindus in free India. Commenting upon this aspect of Jinnah's life, Louis Fischer remarks: "Muslim politicians, playing on the consequent bitterness, told their followers that independence would mean oppression by the Hindu majority, no jobs in government or business, and perhaps compulsory return to Hinduism. These threats Jinnah declared in 1917, were unreal, 'Fear not,' he pleaded, 'this is a bogey which is put before you to scare you away from the co-operation and unity which are essential to self-government.' Yet the bogey could be made to look so real that in the end he himself used it for its usual purpose."[*] As I have already stated, the Congress Party was the only truly representative party of India. It stood for a united India, and its aim was to foster amity between all the communities and to establish a secular democracy. Communal riots had never occurred in the history of India, even when the Muslims ruled the country. They did not even occur prior to the coming into prominence of the Congress Party, which pressed for self-government. The British administrators took advantage of the ignorance of the Indians and adopted all possible means of thwarting the national movement. Fostering fanaticism and creating religious rifts were tactics conducive to British rule. It is said that Jinnah, who left Congress and settled in England as a lawyer, was hired by the British to oppose Gandhi. There is probably some truth in this

---

[*]Louis Fischer, *Gandhi*, p. 80.

theory. Jinnah was elevated by the British administrators, and up to the last minute his fanatic stand, although illogical, divisive and ruinous for India, was supported and ultimately put into effect by the British government. In the beginning the British had only insisted on weight being given to the Muslim League. But just before India got independence Jinnah's Muslim League, which was not representative of all Muslims, insisted on the partition of India on religious grounds. Even if it was ungeographical, unwise, and unjust, the vivisection of India became a real possibility. It might not even have been envisaged by British politicians, who at least in the beginning wanted only to exploit religious differences merely to postpone India's independence. The two-nation theory of Jinnah was completely illogical, virtually insane, and it was never accepted by the Congress Party before and after the partition. Nor was this theory accepted by fifty million Muslims, who still live in India. The undue status given to Jinnah was the sole cause of the absurd and damaging vivisection of India.

I must repeat that Hindus and Muslims in India are simply two of the many communities and not two different nations or cultures. The partition of the Indian nation, therefore, was uncultural and unjust. It led to the economic and political weakness of both India and Pakistan. Whether the blunder was the result of error on the part of Indian politicians or of the machinations of British diplomats, it was disastrous for national and international diplomacy. Lest my own view be deemed prejudicial, I would like to quote Louis Fischer once again in this context. He writes: "The Moslems, who constituted one-fourth of the population of India, and the Hindus, who comprised three fourths, are close kin. Most Moslems of India are converted Hindus, converted by the invading Arabs, Afghans, and Persians who began thrusting into India in the eighth century. Mr. Jinnah said converted Hindus constituted 75 per cent of the Moslem population; Pandit Nehru put it at 95 per cent. In some parts of India, Moslems worship in Hindus temples. In many areas Moslems and Hindus are indistinguishable from one another in appearance, dress, language and custom; Moslems even have castes, like Hindus. Hindi and Urdu, the predominant tongues of Hindus and Moslems, are written with different scripts, and the former has absorbed more Sanskrit words while the latter uses more Persian words, but the two remain very similar. Moreover, in large areas of India, Moslems and Hindus know neither Urdu nor Hindi and have instead a common language—Bengali in Bengal, for instance. Jinnah himself, born in Kathiawar of Hindu ancestry, spoke Gujarati in his father's house, as did Gandhi."*

This is the observation of a foreign visitor. Yet the relations between Indian Muslims and Hindus is even closer than Fischer suggests. About 90 per cent of the Muslims are converts from Hinduism and their customs are totally different from the Muslims of other countries. The state of Punjab in India, which is the result of the partition of the greater Punjab, is the foremost Urdu-speaking state in India. It is noteworthy that the Hindu poets of Urdu in Punjab are highly respected in Pakistan even today. Urdu is the national language of Pakistan and is yet the most popular language of the non-Muslim state of Punjab, where it is still recognized as the language of the law and court. In Pakistan today there is a great controversy between Urdu and Bengali, which is the mother tongue of East Pakistan. The Pakistani Punjabis look down upon the Bengali language and resent the dominance of Bengali-speaking officials in West Pakistan. Thus culturally Pakistan is not different from India, nor were Muslims ever different from the Hindus before the partition.

The purpose of mentioning these facts here is to point out how this irrational and uncalled-for surgical operation upon India, which resulted in the unnecessary dismemberment of a healthy body, hampered the progress of Indian democracy and also that of Pakistani theocracy, ultimately giving advantage to Red China's aggressive designs. The atmosphere of hatred and fanaticism which still dominates Pakistan is disastrous for the progress of a secular democracy, which is India's answer to the creed of totalitarianism.

As long as India was fighting for freedom, and as long as her sons and daughters were subjected to intimidation and violence by the British, not a single member of the Muslim League appeared on the scene. When Congress Party members courted jail and faced dangers and death, the Muslim League was sound asleep. The fact is that Jinnah never expected India to become a free nation. Jinnah's and through him the Muslim League's, was only a dog-in-the-manger policy. They simply wanted what the Congress did not want. They had no policy of their own except that of hindering the progress of the nationalists. The India Act of 1935, which

---

*Ibid., pp. 79-80.

granted provincial autonomy, was the outcome of the sacrifices of the Congress Party, to which the top-ranking Muslims like Maulana Azad, Dr. Ansari, Dr. Kitchlu and the "Frontier Ghandhi," Abdul Ghafar Khan, with millions of his followers, had dedicated their lives. But when the efforts of these self-denying Hindus, Muslims, Sikhs, Christians and Parsis were about to be crowned with success, time-servers like Jinnah and his followers appeared on the scene. They became the self-styled leaders of all the Muslims, when actually the overwhelming majority of Muslims was guided by the nationalist Muslims. The Northwestern Frontier Province, with a population of over eighty per cent Muslims, voted for the Congress Party, and Khan Abdul Ghaffar Khan became the first prime minister of that province.

However, the British policy of supporting the Muslim League continued even after World War II, when the independence of India became imminent. The partition of India into two sovereign states was not, then, the original intention of British politicians, but it was the necessary outcome of their constant policy of encouraging the subversive activities of the Muslim League. India could very easily be declared one independent democratic country when the British decided to withdraw. But just before the event of withdrawal a hurried series of conferences between the British diplomats, Muslim Leaguers, and the Indian National Congress was held. In all these meetings the Muslim League remained obdurate and stuck to the same dog-in-the-manger policy.

Before I discuss the final phase of the birth of Indian democracy, it appears necessary to throw some light on political developments in India immediately before the British took formal leave of the Indian sub-continent. As already stated, the nonviolent mass movement started by Gandhi, which resulted in nation-wide processions and meetings on the part of millions of Indian people and the courting of jail sentences, injury and even death, was the biggest weapon ever used by the Indian National Congress. But Gandhi was very cautious in mobilizing the whole nation. Wherever he launched the satyagraha he issued definite instructions, and the people who joined the movement were aware of Gandhi's sentiments. They knew that the use of any kind of minimal violence to retaliate the excesses of the police would mean the end of satyagraha. The attitude of the Congress was not hostile. Whenever the British government announced political reforms, the Congress usually accepted them under the guidance of Gandhi. It was in this co-operative spirit that after the award of provincial autonomy the Congress Party fought elections and captured the provincial government. Out of eleven provinces only two had a thin majority of the Muslim League. When World War II broke out, India was dragged into it by the British government without any prior consultation with the Indian leaders. The Congress Party was ready to help the war effort on the condition that the British government assure the freedom of the country. But this offer was rejected, because by that time Churchill, who was deadly opposed to Gandhi and Indian independence, had become war-time prime minister. He abhorred the idea of Gandhi, "a half-naked Fakir", meeting the Viceroy of India as the representative of the Indian people. He was perhaps the single greatest obstacle in India's march towards self-government. He was no doubt the greatest man of his country and he was perhaps indispensable for the British people under the circumstances, but judged with reference to the story of Indian independence he was a villain, an enemy of freedom, a ruthless imperialist and the most reactionary Englishman. There is no doubt that he was an open enemy of India's national movement. But he had no reason to be so callous and to exhibit his hatred publicly towards Indian leaders. He refused even to see Gandhi when the latter was in England and was invited by King George to Buckingham Palace. This looks like childishness and certainly does not become one of the greatest men of Britain, which claims to be the sponsor of democracy. Any other person than Gandhi, as the leader of Indian nation, would have retaliated, and such an attitude would have resulted in the permanent dissociation of India and Britain after independence. But Gandhi never said a word to dishonor Churchill.

Gandhi did not only not hate Churchill and Britain, but was really pained to see the British nation in peril of Nazi conquest. When he met Lord Linlithgow, the Viceroy of India during the war, Gandhi was so much overpowered by the emotion of sorrow and sympathy for the possible destruction of the Houses of Parliament and Westminster Abbey in London that he actually shed tears. He denounced Hitlerism, as "naked, ruthless force reduced to an exact science and worked out with scientific precision." He also condemned the Japanese and exhorted his countrymen to beware of the false propaganda let loose by the Japanese with the slogan,

"Asia for the Asiatics." But the sincerity of Gandhi was not heeded by Churchill, who was determined to crush Gandhism and all who supported it by the use of force. On one hand he advocated the cause of freedom and democracy by exhorting people all over the world to hazard all for victory over dictatorship, and on the other hand he detested and dictatorially prevented the freeing of India. His extreme conservatism and his imperialism blinded his judgment and made him the self-styled protector of His Majesty's Empire. There is little doubt that he paid the price for his extreme political views by his downfall just after World War II, but as long as he was in power he disregarded every suggestion for reconciliation with the Indian National Congress and treated the Indian people as the property of the British crown. He disregarded the advice of President Roosevelt, excluded India from the Atlantic Charter, and never budged an inch from his declaration as Prime Minister of Britain, made on November 4, 1942: "I have not become the King's First Minister in order to preside at the liquidation of the British Empire." It was due to this attitude of Churchill that the relations the Congress leaders and the British government deteriorated and the political deadlock continued.

When all doors were closed for negotiation and exchange of views, when the British don't-care attitude passed all limits, Gandhi suggested a mild remedy to remind the British of their callousness towards the Indian people. The remedy was the "Quit India" movement. He suggested that whenever an Indian met a Britisher he should fold his hands in an attitude of prayer and say, "Please quit India." This movement was to be launched all over the country on August 9, 1942. But the British government arrested all the top-ranking leaders, including Gandhi, before the 9th of August dawned. The people were left without any guidance from responsible leaders all over the country. The excesses of the police in all parts of India were retaliated. The socialist Congress leaders came to the fore and a long series of violent clashes between the government and the Indian people began. In many parts of India most means of communication were cut off, government buildings were burnt, and in some places the government was overthrown. These uprisings were dealt with very severely by the government and thousands of Indians were killed. The British government duped the outside world by blaming Gandhi, when actually the callousness and high-handedness of the administration were responsible for the chaos and disorder. Gandhi had suggested negotiations much earlier than his sudden arrest. Had leaders like Nehru, Patel, Azad and others remained out of jail, they would have exercised their moral influence on the masses. But all the responsible patriots were thrown into jail and were physically cut off from their people and from the rest of the world.

This was the last conviction of the Congress leaders, who were released in May of 1944. With the downfall of Churchill and the ascendancy of the Labour party in July, 1945, the Indian leaders became hopeful. During his election campaign Clement Atlee, the Labour Prime Minister, had promised to expedite self-government in India. The Labour government therefore sent a British cabinet mission, whose final report rejected the partition of India on quite rational grounds. The Muslim League, which had by now been given equal status with the Congress Party, again adopted the most obstinate attitude and insisted on the creation of an impracticable Pakistan in which 52 per cent Muslims would govern 48 per cent non-Muslims in six provinces of India. One theory is that Jinnah was still in league with reactionary British people and was guided by their advice. There is considerable plausibility in this theory. The recognition of the Muslim league as the sole champion of all Muslims of India was unjust when millions of Muslims were in fact under the leadership of patriots like Maulana Azad, Dr. Ansari, Dr. Kitchlu and Khan Abdul Ghaffar Khan, who had established a purely Congress government in the purely Muslim area of the Northwestern Frontier province. The Labour government might have been sincere, and probably was sincere in its dealing with the situation. But Jinnah's irrational demand and his repeated slogans could not have been merely the result of his own thinking. If it is true that he secretly sought guidance from anti-Labour elements in Britain, it would have been wiser for the Labour government to overlook such a selfish fanatic leader.

Before I proceed to describe the tense atmosphere created by the Muslim league to force the partition, I would like to give here the view of a Western observer about the unjustified stand of Jinnah, the unrivalled leader of the reactionary Muslim League, which died its own death in its self-created theocratic Pakistan after causing great harm to the Indian subcontinent. Commenting upon the demand of Jinnah for Pakistan this writer says: "In any case, the bisection of India on Jinnah's terms was impossible and unjust. He wanted Pakistan so that Hindus would not rule over Moslems. But Assam, which he demanded for Pakistan, had only 3,442,479 Moslems as against 6,762,254 non-Moslems. In the vast Punjab province, the Moslems numbered 16,217,242, non-Moslems 12,201,577. In Bengal with about sixty million inhabitants, Moslems constituted 52 per cent, little more than half. In these three regions alone, if they were included in Pakistan, fifty million Moslems would rule over forty-seven million Hindus and Sikhs. Pakistan would be born with a leaden minority problem around its infant neck. At the same time, Jinnah's proposed Pakistan left twenty million Moslems, or one-fifth of India's Moslems, under Hindu rule. Yet Jinnah was deaf to logic and blind to arithmetic. Irrational resoluteness, even when it conflicts with self-interest, nevertheless often makes history."*

The fact remains that Jinnah did not really want to serve the cause of religion or even the cause of all the Muslims, whom he falsely claimed to be his followers. He wanted only to exploit religious sentiments and to carve out a state in which he should rule supreme as the Quaid-E-Azam, or Great Apostle of Morality. He himself was not at all a true Muslim. Contrary to the tenets of Islam he drank wine and ate pork. He was westernized and could not speak or read Urdu, the national language of Pakistan. He married a non-Muslim Parsi girl of eighteen when he was forty years old. But he was intelligent and he knew how to exploit the religious sentiments of the illiterate masses, even though he himself did not very often come in direct touch with them. Unfortunately the people who followed him did not give much thought to the consequences of a theocratic state. Let me quote here again the same western author, who says, "Interviewing Jinnah was like listening to a cracked phonograph record, no argument, merely endless repetition of slogans, 'Hindus and Moslems Are Separate Nations'; 'Gandhi Wants Hindu Raj'; 'Pakistan Must Be.' This single-minded fanaticism, unreasoning poison, and unbounded hate . . . had an enormous appeal to the people whose hard lives and frustration made them an easy prey to simple goals charged with emotion . . . The victims of Jinnah were as oblivious as he to the mathematics of minorities and to practical considerations. He gave them an intoxicating banner: Pakistan. He thought only of achieving

---

*Ibid., pp. 49-50.

Pakistan, never of the problems of Pakistan. In fact for the first few years after he broached the idea, he even refused to indicate the future borders of Pakistan. The less concrete the project, the more fascinating and the less attainable by criticism. The situation was a fanatic's paradise."**

The two-nation theory of Jinnah was never accepted by the Congress Party, which continued to be the sole representative of all communities and which constantly aimed at a secular democracy. Pampered by the British and proud of his unrivalled position in the Muslim League, Jinnah could claim a thin majority of Muslim Leaguers in only two out of eleven provinces up to February of 1947. And yet it was his two-nation theory which was accepted by the British and which led to the partition of India, leaving fifty million Muslims in secular India until today. How did this happen? How did the apparently irrational plan become a reality? This is the question which again requires us to refer to events just before the birth of Indian democracy. These are the events which were planned and thrashed out at secret meetings of the Muslim League. They were not known to the Congress leaders and the details are not known even today.

The Muslim League, with Jinnah as its permanent chief, propagated religious fanaticism through various organizations. Its activities became prominent after 1935 when Jinnah, who had been living in England as a lawyer, returned to India, for he could sense that the India Act of 1935 was the forerunner of Indian freedom. His aims were to put obstacles in the way of Congress, to mislead the Muslim masses by harping on the two-nation theory, and to capture power. He failed to capture political power in the Northwest Frontier province, the province having the highest percentage of Muslims. Similiarly the Muslim League returned a negligible minority in the elections in Punjab, the province which was the stronghold of the activities of the Muslim league and of which Lahore, the erstwhile capital of Punjab, was the geographical center. It is noteworthy that until February, 1947, the Punjab was ruled by the Unionist party, a coalition of non-Congress Hindus and non-Muslim League Muslims.

In 1946, when the Interim Federal Government was established, with Nehru as Prime Minister, it became evident that India would

---

**Ibid., pp. 52-53.

be free within a year. At first the Muslim League refused to join Nehru's cabinet, but later on it got into it. The subversive tactics of the Muslim League not only continued, but were redoubled. The Leaguers were furious because Punjab was being governed by a non-Muslim League party. I happen to come from Punjab and was friendly with the leading Muslim Leaguers of my town. In 1946, the Muslim League hoped to capture power in Punjab by fair means or foul. It wanted influential leaders. It had become conscious that freedom was knocking at the door of India and that Unionist party rule in Punjab was a blot on the prestige of the Muslim League. I remember attending a public meeting of the Muslim League, where I was the only Hindu present owing to my friendly relations with the local Muslim leaders. Hindus were afraid of attending any public meetings of the Muslim League in Punjab because the speeches made by the fanatic Leaguers very often provoked the masses and resulted in rioting and the killing of Hindus in those days. This particular gathering of about twenty thousand was addressed by Mr. Feroz Khan Noon, who had been the non-Muslim League Minister of Punjab for a long time, and who had recently returned from Europe. He was first eulogised by the local illiterate but most fanatic leader of the Muslim League, whose previous fiery speeches in the local dialect must be credited with having caused several riots in the town. This leader, who had been baptized by the local Muslim League papers as the "uncrowned king" of that town, compared Sir Feroz Khan Noon to the sun (the word 'Feroz' means sun). Then he condemned the Unionist government of Punjab in the filthiest language he could utter. He abused Nehru, praised Jinnah, and received great applause from the crowd, which rent the air with the loud slogan, "Le Ke Rahenge Pakistan" . . . "Pakistan we will surely acquire." This occasion was the conversion of Sir Feroz Khan Noon as a new member of the Muslim League. The 'uncrowned king' of the town said in his speech, "Now the sword of Sir Feroz Khan Noon, the sun of Punjab, will kill the Hindus, the Aharar party (a very popular non-Muslim League Muslim party of Punjab) and the Unionist government led by Mr. Khizar Hayat Khan (the then prime minister of Punjab)." He used alliteration while uttering the three enemies of the Muslim League in his native dialect. He said that the Muslims of Punjab should remember that they had three foes to fight, "Kirar (Hindus), Ahrar (the Ahrar party), and

Khizari Garkar (the government of Khizar Hayat Khan)." He was warmly cheered by the huge crowd when he uttered the alliteration and then added, "Against these we have our Ferozi Talwar (the sword of Sir Feroz Khan Noon)." Sir Feroz Khan Noon, acknowledging the tribute paid to him, said in reply that he had come to his country from Europe because he had been informed by the British authorities in England that the independence of India was drawing near, and that now was the most opportune time for the Muslims to unite under the Islamic banner and to press for an independent state of Pakistan.

It is noteworthy that the top-ranking leaders of the Muslim League and the sponsors of the idea of Pakistan were almost all title holders, Sirs, Nawabs, and recipients of land from the British government. Sir Mohhamad Iqbal is supposed to be the first person to have generated the idea of a monolithic state and to have coined the word "Pakistan," which literally means "the pure land." Such big landlords and Nawabs, who were the honored courtiers of the deputy commissioner, the ruler of the district, could cause communal riots in their areas on a moment's notice. That is why I think that the theory which suggests that the Muslim League was secretly fostered by reactionary British diplomats and bureaucrats holds good, and obviously confirms the theory that the British policy of "divide and rule" reigned supreme in India until she attained independence.

Causing riots, arson, looting, knifing and hooliganism were the methods adopted by the Muslim League to scare the Hindus, to make them feel that they were not secure in the Muslim majority provinces, and to intimidate the Congress to accept the creation of Pakistan. There is no doubt that the plans for these subversive activities were drafted at secret meetings of the Muslim League, and the organized mass-killing of the Hindus and Sikhs in Punjab before and after the partition was a part of the game successfully played by the Muslim League. The activities of the League behind the scene are overlooked by those Western observers who sometimes wrongly blame India for various issues between her and Pakistan. When in 1946 the Muslim League entered the Interim government and made attempts to sabotage the administration at every step, the Congress became cautious and also suspicious of the intentions of Jinnahites. I am tempted again to quote Louis Fischer on this point. Referring to the intentions of the Muslim League he says,

"Liaquat Ali Khan, the foremost of the League members of the government, frankly stated that they did not recognize Nehru's government as the government of India and felt under no obligation to co-operate with it. Nor did they join to sabotage it."*

When the Muslim Leaguers could not succeed in sabotaging the Federal government due to the vigilance of the Congress members, they set to work their destructive machinery of rioting and killing Hindus mercilessly in Bengal, which was ruled by the Muslim League government. The disorder and chaos, which involved mass killing, arson, looting and rape of Hindu women by the blood-thirsty Muslims of Noakhali and Trihura, the two regions of Bengal province, were the result of the "direct action" announced by the Muslim League to protest against the Interim government. It is most important to note that this trouble started in Bengal, where the Muslim League government was in power. Soon the trouble spread to Punjab, where the Unionist ministry had voluntarily handed over the right of the government to the Muslim League. Again it is noteworthy that riots and mass killing started in Punjab just after the Muslim League flag was flown on the Legislative Assembly building in Lahore, the capital of Punjab. This wildfire before the announcement of the partition of India on June 3, 1947, was in fact a prelude to the tragic drama which was to be staged just after August 15, 1947, in West Pakistan, to turn out—or rather to kill—all Hindus and Sikhs unless they were converted to Islam. We who were living in that area knew it or at least apprehended it. The Muslim League, in the whole of Punjab and in Delhi, had secretly created arsenals of firearms and other lethal weapons and proceeded to use them. When the affected areas, presenting the horrible scenes of burnt buildings and the decaying dead bodies of thousands of men, women and children were visited by Lord Mountbatten and Nehru, it was brought to their notice that those happenings were the plan and work of the Muslim League. But the people who mattered did not doubt the bonafides of the Muslim League as a political body.

Neither Hinduism, nor Islam, nor Sikhism, nor Christianity as a religion preaches hatred. Islam believes in loving neighbors, as does Christianity and Hinduism. God is not the monopoly of one community or nation or continent or even of one planet. He is

---

*Ibid., p. 161.

recognized as the God of the universe, of the whole creation. God does not belong only to Hindus or Christians or Muslims or Sikhs or Jews, but to all mankind. A Muslim has to pray five times a day, and that prayer contains the phrase, "Rubul Alamin," i.e., "God of all the creatures of the universe." It reminds a Muslim five times a day that God is not the monopoly of Muslims. Had it been so the prayer would have read, "Rabul Musalimin," the God of Muslims. According to the tenets of Islam, "a true Muslim or Moman is he who has respect for all revealed religions." If he disregards any other revealed religion, then according to Islam he is not a Muslim. How universal is the belief of God in Islam? Hinduism likewise believes in the universal brotherhood of human beings, as the children of the same God. Yet all sorts of atrocities, arson, murders, crimes and cruelties were done in the name of religion by the so-called sponsors of religion. If the Muslim Leaguers exploited the ignorance of true Islam on the part of the Muslim masses, the Hindus who retaliated also acted against their own religion. As a matter of fact, it was not religion which prompted the Muslims to attack and the Hindus and Sikhs to retaliate but the very negation of religion, the thirst for power, the lust for overlordship and political self-aggrandizement. Misunderstandings arise only when we do not know our religion truly. "Islam in danger" was the slogan of those who did not know what Islam stood for.

Whatever might have been the root cause of the fanaticism, it did take a heavy toll of life and even the most staunch nationalist leaders had under these special circumstances to yield to the partition of India. It was announced that India would be made independent on the 15th of August, 1947, and that on the same day two sovereign states, India and Pakistan, would come into existence. Mahatma Gandhi was the sole person who would not agree to the partition. But the Congress party accepted it; Jinnah, the generator of Pakistan, pounced upon it, and the departing British government sanctioned and legalized it.

But before the date of independence arrived, the drama of genocide was enacted, and in the West Pakistan area, arson, looting, murder and rape were rampant. The exchange of population became imminent in Punjab and Sindh. A train of the Hindu and Sikh refugees, which started from Lahore (now in Pakistan) for Amritsar in the East Punjab part of India, was detained by the fanatic Muslims and its thousands of occupants were butchered, to the last man, woman and child. A similar treatment was meted out to a train of Muslim refugees on the Amritsar side of the border by the Hindus and Sikhs. These two heinous acts stopped possible future butchering of refugees on both sides. Every safe arrival of a train of the Hindu and Sikh refugees in India was exchanged by a similar safe arrival of a train of Muslim refugees in Pakistan. Miles long processions of refugees, walking on foot, entered India and Pakistan, weeping and crying, tired and hungry with their infants in their arms. But as soon as they reached India or Pakistan they cheered themselves with the slogans, "Long live India," or "Long live Pakistan." The birth of the twin states of India and Pakistan, therefore, was celebrated with mixed emotions of joy and sorrow, pleasure and pain, and hope and disappointment on August 15, 1947, in New Delhi and Karachi, the capitals of India and Pakistan respectively. Thus was born the Indian democracy, with its faith in a secular state, a state where persons belonging to all religions and communities, all races and castes, would have equal opportunity in politics and in the economy, in government service and administration, in private enterprise, business and industry. But the achievement of this ideal involved heavy responsibilities, tremendous tasks and vast problems without solving which the administration could collapse any day and its hard won independence disappear in a moment.

CHAPTER IV

Insoluble Problems

The achievement of political independence, especially under the circumstances mentioned in the previous chapter, is not sufficient for the establishment of a strong and secular democracy in a nation which had for centuries been subjected to slavery. On the contrary, freedom is a great handicap and even a danger when the essential ingredients of democracy—literacy, political awakening, economic stability and freedom from prejudice and superstition—are lacking. Communism, as I have already said, steps in when chaos and disorder, hatred and jealousy, ignorance and poverty frustrate the individual. All these symptoms in the worst possible form were present in the newborn democracy of India, and a lack of dexterity, integrity and acumen in the builders of the Indian nation could have very easily led either to civil war or to Communism. The insoluble problems were those of the rehabilitation of tens of millions of refugees, the avoidance of armed conflict with Pakistan, the maintenance of the political unity of India as a secular nation in the presence of the fanatic propaganda of theocratic Pakistan, which was constantly driving non-Muslims from its territory, and the problem of five hundred and sixty-two princely states, whose rulers had the full power to exercise their discretion to remain independent units or to merge with either of the two sovereign states, India and Pakistan.

The foremost problem was that of the refugees from both Pakistans, East and West. But the refugees from West Pakistan were more numerous. The evacuation of these millions of people was itself a great problem. All the railway trains of Northern India, all the buses and trucks and all the aeroplanes of the government and private companies were engaged in bringing panic-stricken

41

people from Pakistan with little or no luggage, food or clothing on their person. Most had literally run away from their hearths and homes to save their lives, leaving all their valuables, money and ornaments in Pakistan. Many of those who made attempts to bring money or gold ornaments were robbed of their belongings at the border by the Muslims. Pakistani officers would not allow the evacuating non-Muslims to take out any valuables. The result was that millions of refugees had to be accommodated in huge camps and supplied with food and clothing. A new ministry of Relief and Rehabilitation was immediately created, and hundreds of millions of rupees were spent to rehabilitate these oppressed, displaced persons.

The work of evacuation continued for several months after the partition and during those months there were no regular railway trains or buses running between Delhi and the partitioned part of Punjab. It took several days for a person to travel two hundred miles. I remember taking seventeen days when in the month of October, 1947, I went from Ganganagar in the princely state of Bikaner to the border town of Amritsar to receive my parents who had been evacuated from Pakistan by air. The distance between these two cities was only about two hundred and fifty miles. I had to travel by train, by bus, by truck and on foot. The freight trains were also being used for passengers, but they sometimes stopped at various stations on the way for a week or so. There was complete chaos in communications. Hundreds of thousands of refugees—men, women, and children—were seen sleeping on the roadside, in the open fields, and on the footpaths in the towns of Punjab through which I passed. Railway trains carrying the refugees were overloaded far beyond safety limits. Thousands of passengers travelled on the tops of the trains, and there were hundreds of accidental deaths owing to the abnormal mode of travel.

More dangerous than hunger was the anger of refugees who had suffered untold miseries and many of whom had lost their kith and kin in Pakistan. Thousands of widows and orphans, whose husbands or parents had been murdered, bemoaned and bewailed their fate, and their relations, who had rescued them from Pakistan, angrily blamed the Congress government. They demanded revenge and wanted all Muslims from India sent to Pakistan. Rashtriya Svayam Sewak Sangh, a purely Hindu organization which had physically fought the Muslims in Pakistan and had saved hundreds of thousands of Hindus, became more important for these wronged refugees than the Congress Party. People simply forgot that it was the Congress government which had placed all the means of communication and the military at the disposal of the refugees for their safe evacuation. When their emotions were aroused, their reason was overpowered, and there was no room for cool contemplation on the pros and cons of a solution. To the Punjabis who are known for their emotional nature, banishment from their native land to which they were attached was the severest emotional shock. It was natural for such people to fume and fret and to condemn the Congress Party, which being a truly national organization, had Muslim cabinet ministers and high officials both in the provinces and at the center of government. These infuriated refugees asked how Congress was justified in allowing Muslims to rule over Hindus when these very Hindus had been butchered and turned out from the state of Pakistan. Why should not all Muslims be forced to go to their theocratic state? Why should they have their cake and eat it too? They demanded the evacuation of Muslims from India and threatened to kill all Muslims in Delhi and in the neighboring states. Not only the refugees, but many of the inhabitants of Punjab, Rajasthan and Uttar Pradesh, who gave refuge to millions of these displaced persons, began to feel the same way.

It was very difficult to convince these people, much less to intimidate them by the use of force or political power. The only way open to the Congress government was to solve the problem of rehabilitation of the refugees, and to be sympathetic with the people who had been forced to leave their hearths and homes, people who had literally sacrificed everything for the sake of the freedom of India. But at the same time it was also most important to maintain law and order, to safeguard the life of every Muslim in India, and to bring civil life back to normal. When riots broke out in Delhi, as a repercussion of the constant provocation caused by the atrocities committed in Pakistan, it was discovered that in many Muslim mosques there were secret arsenals whose stores were used in the riots to kill Hindus. But during the exchange of populations, the Muslims were in a minority, and the protection of minorities is the first duty of a just government. The protection of minorities was the protection of the secular democracy, and the protection of a secular democracy was the protection of freedom. Had Congress deviated from the secular and nationalist ideal it would have been doomed as a political organization, and India, like Pakistan, might have become a theocratic state, the very negation of democracy.

In the midst of all this high emotion, Gandhi, the father of the nation, stuck to reason; in the midst of high tension he was calm and composed. He continued to bring home to the masses and leaders the importance of communal harmony and the maintenance of law and order. He said that India ought to stick to its secular ideal, irrespective of the fanaticism prevailing in Pakistan. The problem was how to calm the millions of people and to make them feel the necessity of national unity, when fire was raging in Pakistan and even Sindh was being evacuated by the Hindus under duress? The riots in the capital had been controlled but tension continued. When a dump of ammunition was discovered in some Muslim locality, tension increased. It appeared that normality would never return to the capital of India. No physical force could quell the feeling of the people, who having been uprooted from their native places found that even in free India, for which they had sacrificed everything, they were not welcomed. They thought that they were wronged when the government not only protected the Muslims but did not encourage or force them to go to Pakistan as refugees. Pakistan had used all possible means to harass the Hindus; the police and the military had encouraged the Muslim masses to indulge in rioting and genocide. The policy of the Pakistan government was to purge the whole country of non-Muslims, and to usurp the entire property of Hindus and Sikhs. But the Indian government had no such intentions. It did not only protect the life and property of the Muslims in India, but it also helped the Pakistan government to make a good start by liberally paying it five hundred and fifty million rupees from the Indian treasury. Gandhi went on a fast and said that he would not break it until Delhi was free from communal tension. This vow of Gandhi had an almost magical effect on the masses. The refugees did not want the father of the nation to suffer for them. They forgot their woes and came forward to help the government to bring normality to Delhi. They embraced the Muslims and inaugurated processions with Muslims demonstrating communal harmony. Gandhi was satisfied and broke his fast. Thus the problem of restoring peace in the capital was not solved by force but by love.

However, as I have already stated, events before and after the partition which were not expected even by the most sagacious politicians of India did make Congress unpopular among the illiterate masses. There was a perceptible inclination among the Hindus who had witnessed the miseries of the refugees to blame Congress for complacency and an appeasement policy towards the Muslims. Muslims demanded Pakistan and they got it, hence they had no right to continue to enjoy special privileges in India. This was the trend of thinking among many people, and the prestige of Congress was at its lowest ebb. Gandhi suggested that Congress should cease to be a political body and should engage itself in nation-building activities in real service to the people of India. He felt that after the attainment of independence it was more important to educate the masses of India to become responsible citizens of a democracy, to unite, and to work hard to drive out poverty. Although the trend of underestimating the worth of the Congress party was not yet a massive one, yet it was gaining ground, and particularly the Rashtriya Svayam Sewak Sangh, which was becoming very popular in those days, appeared to be the organization which might take over in a change of government. Gandhi, however, did not mean that the Congress party was incapable of governing the country. He honestly wanted Congress to undertake the nation-building work. But the feeling among the Hindu masses was different. Many appeared to have lost confidence in the Congress and this feeling was a great challenge not only to Congress but to the survival of secular democracy in India. Had that feeling gained ground, had a fanatically communal party taken charge of the Indian government at that time, dictatorship and not democracy, totalitarianism and not freedom would have been the creed of India.

This situation, which is now only a forgotten event of history, perhaps even unrecorded by the academic historian, was the most crucial and the most critical situation faced by this nation at the dawn of its freedom. The Rashtriya Syayam Sewak Sangh, whose aim was to unite the Hindus and to make them physically stronger to repel and revenge Muslim violence, expected the deterioration of the communal crisis in India. In those days, even after the evacuation of the Hindu refugees was accomplished, this organization expected the spread of communal riots and was secretly preparing to meet the expected violence on the part of Muslims, who were reported to have organized themselves all over India. The sudden attack of Pakistan on Kashmir confirmed these doubts, and the Muslims in India were held to be the fifth column of Pakistan. This was a widespread apprehension and it undermined the prestige of the Congress in the minds of the people. I do not agree with those who think that Rashtriya Svayam Sevak Sangh was conspiring against Congress. Its activities in those days were defensive and it had played a heroic role in defending the Hindus and Sikhs in Pakistan. I do not agree with the concept of an all-Hindu nation, or Hindu Raj, which is a concept prejudicial to democracy, and I do not know whether any political party in India except the communal body, the Hindu Maha Sabha, ever thought of a Hindu Raj. If the Rashtriya Svayam Sevak Sangh had wished to enter politics with the idea of establishing a purely Hindu government like Pakistan, it could have declared itself to be a political body. But it did not do so. Whatever might have been the intentions and the political implications of the activities of R.S.S.S. in those days, it is well-known that this organization did save the lives of millions of Hindus and Sikhs during the disturbances in Pakistan. Those who witnessed the ruthless attacks of the Muslims in the towns and villages of Punjab and who had been rescued by R.S.S.S. volunteers, could not but admire the bravery of its followers. The police and even the military in Pakistan area would not check the Muslim attackers and death stared the Hindu victims in the face. On such occasions the R.S.S.S. volunteers, who had been trained and organized as disciplined soldiers, often came to the rescue of frightened Hindus and Sikhs and repulsed the Muslim attacks even by using crude bombs. The attackers were much larger in number and the Hindus within city walls were fewer. But the exploding of a crude bomb scared the attackers, and they dared not enter the cities. For several days the Hindus could keep the attackers away until the military from India could evacuate them. Thus the first-aid defense measures provided by the R.S.S.S. were admired, and it was thought that this organization had great utility.

However, this growing admiration for the R.S.S.S. was dangerous insofar as it undermined the prestige of a national body like Congress, which stood for a secular democracy. Unfortunately the admiration was continuously increasing and the rumor began that some top-ranking Congress leaders were also secretly fostering this organization. These unfounded rumors had great propaganda value and might have brought about havoc or even a coup. I do not know whether the Congress leaders were conscious of the gravity of the situation or not. But they did have full faith in the ideals of Gandhi and Congress. They certainly opposed the communal clashes and made honest efforts to restore law and order. The question was how to bring confidence back to the masses. The Muslims were certainly scared, though they were protected; the Hindus were doubtful, and R.S.S.S. expected violence on the part of the Indian Muslims. This was the darkest period, the most critical period of fluctuation between hope and fear, courage and doubt, and between confidence and diffidence. Perhaps Gandhi could have made a whirlwind tour to inspire confidence, to invoke love and brotherhood and to "lead kindly light amidst the encircling gloom." He had already declared that he would now go to Pakistan and spend the rest of his life there. It was a very important declaration, the wisest declaration, perhaps the most fateful step which Gandhi was to take. But before this apostle of peace and love could execute this plan, the gloomiest hour of India arrived. A neurotic, misled by ignorance and hate, and upset by the idea of India's financial succor to Pakistan, committed the crime of paying love by hatred to the promoter of the maxim "Return love for hatred." Gandhi, perhaps the most harmless human being ever born in the last century, who literally and actually loved his enemy, was made the target of the three fatal bullets of a fanatic Hindu, Nathuram Godse, who had neither suffered as a refugee, nor was related to any person migrating from Pakistan. Gandhi paid the heaviest price for freedom. He laid down his life smilingly, not retaliating or even trying to push away his assailant or avoiding the bullets by crouching down, but by blessing his murderer and uttering the name of God three times before he succumbed. How could he have proved truer to his words, uttered a few decades before his death, "I will die as a soldier"? How could he also prove truer to his promise, "Pakistan would be built on my bones"? The light was put out, but before being extinguished it enkindled the hearts of his people. His death was a tribute to the freedom of India, a sacrifice for the resoration of love, brotherhood and unity among Indians. Refugees as well as non-refugees, Hindus, Muslims, Sikhs and Christians all realized "how dangerous it is to be too good," and how fanaticism and communalism can kill the most innocent, the most pious, humane and loving, and the most honest democrat like Gandhi. If Gandhi could be murdered by a fanatic, what about the fate of others? This was an alarm. Gandhi died, but with him also died the misgivings about the bonafides of Congress among the Indians. Gandhi's blood nourished the ideals of the Congress, restored confidence in the minds of the fluctuating Indians and set them on the path of a secular democracy. Gandhi had to die sooner or later. But his death at the most critical moment when India needed his guidance was most painful and at the same time most significant. It answered the question, "Should India adopt a secular democracy or a Hindu theocracy?" Gandhi lived and died for the unity of India. His death like his life inspired the Congress leaders to march on the path of democratic progress with greater strength and courage, vigor and confidence. Gandhi's glorious death therefore was a blessing in disguise and it made Indian independence a most valuable thing, the dearest heritage worth protecting, because its price was paid by the life of a man who had awakened the Indians from their slavish slumber and brought them priceless freedom. The insoluble communal problem was solved and the democratic elements emerged stronger and brighter in Indian society than ever before.

Civil war, which might have been the result of communal fanaticism, was avoided. But there was another knotty problem created by the anomalous clause of the covenant between the five hundred and sixty-two princely states and the British government. According to this covenant, I have pointed out, the British government had given a free choice to the princely states either to join India or Pakistan or to declare themselves independent. The power of exercising this choice was vested in the ruler of every state. How damaging was this clause to prove in the charter of Indian independence? Suppose all these rulers had unanimously declared themselves sovereign after the sovereignty of the British crown was lifted in 1947, what would have been the consequences? If communal civil war was averted by India's not coming into armed conflict with Pakistan, the danger of regional civil war was still there, at least potentially. The British gave us not only a truncated free India, but also an India with the potentialities of political explosions at every step. If all these explosives had blown up simultaneously and an internecine civil war started, Indians in the midst of chaos and disorder would perhaps have requested the British to stage an honorable return to restore law and order. Could that not be the part of the political game? This is a question which demands a searching of hearts. I am not particularly concerned here to answer this question, nor has it any political significance today. But I am trying to point out that Indian politicians who had to tackle the initial problems of free India were justified in being skeptical even after the British left India. Allowance for this skepticism must be made while judging the behavior of Indians towards the Western democracies, including America, during the formative years of the Indian democracy. India had the bitterest experience of Imperialism and it therefore was justified in remaining non-aligned with any power bloc, Russian or Western. Imperialism was gone, but the royal families and autocrat rulers of states were still there. They were there with full power of exercising their will even to be sovereign. The British government never gave them this choice as long as it ruled India. This choice was given only to allow them to sting the national government if they wanted to.

However, it is true that defense and foreign affairs were not in these princes' hands. The British government had always centrally controlled the military power in India. Though many of these rulers did have their own armies they were not large enough to declare an open war against the new India. However, if they had declared themselves sovereign, they could have created more than a nuisance, possibly a small-scale war. They could no doubt dictate terms if they so desired. They had their own union called "The Chamber of Princes" and could have expressed their opinion forcibly through this organization. Luckily, we had a very strong man as Home Minister at that time. He was Sardar Vallabh Bhai Patel, known as the "iron man of India." Gandhi had full confidence in Patel's will power and in his subtle judgment. If the Indian National Government had a mind to take over all these states by force, it could have been accomplished at a moment's notice. The Congress knew it, the people knew it, and the princes also knew it. But Congress, the votary of truth and non-violence, would certainly abhor the idea of using force against the Indians, whether aristocrats or democrats, classes or masses, or kings or commoners. This was a truism which made these princes fearless and confident. Patel negotiated and addressed their conferences, offered them honorable terms and finally gave them full freedom to decide what to do. Luckily again, good sense prevailed. One after the other, all the states joined either India or Pakistan with the exception of

Kashmir and Hyderabad, the former being on the border of India and Pakistan, and the latter being a complete island in India.

I will return to the problem of Kashmir in the sequel, but I may add here that when a fantically communal Muslim organization called Razakars threatened the peace of Hyderabad and attempted to revive the riots, arson, looting, etc. in the island state (it was surrounded by Indian democratic areas), the police action against this threat brought about the merger of this state with India within two days. The merger of all these states which were geographically as well as culturally part of India was a herculean task but it was accomplished within a few weeks after attaining freedom.

This difficult problem having been solved successfully, there were other hurdles. These princely states, as I have already mentioned, were always ruled by princes whose whim was law. According to the covenant of the merger, these rulers enjoyed the privileges of governing their subjects autocratically. However, some states immediately introduced popular governments and appointed the local Congress leaders as ministers in their cabinets. But these states were so numerous and some of them so small that even the establishment of separate democratic government in them was unwise. Patel gave thought to this problem and suggested the formation of larger states with the voluntary merger of the smaller states. His scheme was happily accepted, and within seven months after the attainment of independence all these princely states had popular government on the pattern of the provincial governments in the rest of India. Gradually all the states joined one or the other group of the merged states and the differences between the princely states and the provincial states disappeared in a short time. By March of 1949 all rulers of these states voluntarily relinquished ruling powers and handed over the rights of the government to the popular ministers responsible to the state assemblies, thereby substituting for autocratic rule a "government of the people, for the people, and by the people."

This was the progress of democracy, the evolutionary democracy, as opposed to violent and revolutionary Communism which was rejected by Indians before and after independence. I will point out further how the success of democracy in India worked as a bulwark against Communism and helped India to advance economically, politically and socially. What I wish to point out here is the prevalence of love and understanding in India as opposed to hatred and misunderstanding. I must here pay tribute to the patriotism of the princes, the hereditary rulers, who had for centuries, in some cases for millenia, been the masters of territories and had been worshipped by their subjects virtually as gods. The spirit of self-sacrifice on their part is commendable and the example of voluntary abdication from kingdoms on their part is an unprecedented event in human history. This bloodless revolution, this real victory of love and non-violence sounds like fiction. But this is what happened in India and this is what testifies to the influence of the deep-rooted culture and religion of the Indian people on their practical life.

CHAPTER V

Progress of Democracy

"Nothing succeeds like success" is an old, but significant proverb. The pragmatic testing of an ideology is essential, for if a plan of living fails to lead a society towards development and progress, if it falls short of its hopes and ambitions, its targets and goals, that theory or plan is bound to be rejected and repudiated. The unprecedented political experiment of democracy in India has withstood the pragmatic test and it has proved to be a satisfactory and promising plan of life to its Indian adherents who initially were handicapped in many respects. We should not forget that in spite of its rich and varied cultural background, the Indian masses were cut off from the world as long as this country was under the subjugation of a foreign power. I have already indicated how illiteracy was the order of the day when the British left India. But in spite of this illiteracy and lack of touch with scientific progress and technical research, the Indian illiterate masses have pragmatically proved that a democratic way of life is pregnant with good results.

Long before her attaining independence, it was held that literacy was the minimum prerequisite for the success of democracy in India. When the British ruled India they advanced this argument in defense of their refusal to grant independence to the Indian people. They pointed out to the free world outside India that hardly eight percent of Indians were literate and that any sort of self government granted to India would be a virtual mess and political chaos. Yet the same illiterate masses in India have successfully gone through three general elections on the basis of an unconditional adult franchise. Does that not falsify the notion that literacy is a prerequisite for exercising a franchise in a democracy? The Indian masses may have been illiterate but they were never uneducated. Education is different from literacy and should not be confused with it. Education is not mere acquaintance with reading, writing and arithmatic. It is in fact the development or the enlargement of mind. Education means getting knowledge through experience; it means an all 'round development of personality through human contact and practical application of ideals. Moreover, education should not be identified or confused with Western education. When the British conquered India politically, they also wanted to conquer it culturally. But they could not suppress Hindu culture, which was potentially democratic. The survival of Indian culture, in spite of its political subjugation, kept the common man in India in constant touch with his traditions. India had a democratic structure of society in the hoary past and that structure was present in its traditions. It was this unwritten law of traditions which helped the adoption of a democratic constitution in India. I will return to the cultural aspect of Indian democracy in the sequel. What I would like to point out here is that although illiteracy and ignorance of the modern concept of democracy were great handicaps to India, they were not serious enough to discourage the adoption of democracy and the granting of an adult franchise.

There is no doubt that literacy and education in the Western sense of the term are being accepted in India. But freedom and democracy could not wait for this transformation. Had India remained deprived of freedom because its people were illiterate, there could have been no political consciousness and no drive for adopting the democratic way of life. Ignorance would have led to the acceptance of subjugation, and subjugation would never have given them a chance to be educated, thus creating a vicious circle. Gandhi wanted to break this circle. He urged that the illiterates be given the chance to, try democracy and he had an implicit faith in the capability of the teeming millions of India to adopt democracy. The adoption of democratic decentralization, which has brought self-government to all the villages of India, has proved, successful. In this chapter, therefore, I would like to illuminate the problem of illiteracy versus democracy and discuss the adoption of democratic decentralization in India. I shall try to show how Indian democracy has made headway in spite of vast educational and social handicaps. This progress is chiefly responsible for the affirmation of faith in democracy on the part of the Indians and for the rejection of the dangerous alternative of communism.

Many Western scholars have over-emphasized the impact of the West, especially of Britain, on India and have suggested that India would not have adopted democracy if the British had not governed that country. I do not want to commit the fallacy of totally refuting this view and then of going to the other extreme and holding that the British did not influence India's political and social life at all. What I wish to point out is that British influence was not so laudable, well-intentioned or effective to be the basis and background of Indian democracy. On the contrary I feel that if India had been made independent a few decades earlier than 1947, she would have been much better off than she is today. If the mere presence of the British as rulers had been a passport to political progress, then all the British-held colonies would have equally thrived. India did gain from the British because she had the potentiality to do so. She already had a rich and varied culture, a way of life which once had been the expression of a unique ideal of "unity in diversity." India also made commendable economic progress in the hoary past. A careful study would reveal that this country was materially progressive and economically sound. Speaking of the prosperity of India in ancient times, Radhakrishanan says, "She developed all arts, fine and industrial, which furnished the conditions of civilized existence. Her conceptions of man and society, morals and religions were remarkable for the time. We cannot reasonably say that the Indian people revelled in poetry and mythology, and spurned science and philosophy, though it is true that they were more bent on seeking unity of things than emphasizing their sharpness and separation." How Indian philosophy aimed at the integrated development of the individual and of the society, and how the dignity of man was the most important truth with the Indian thinkers from hoary past to the present day, I will discuss at the proper place. What I want the reader to become aware of is that India's adoption of democracy was not a mere accident, certainly not the mere accident of having been governed by the British people.

Gandhi did inspire confidence in the minds of the masses of India. He did so not because he was educated in England but because he was a true Indian. He did not only speak the language of the peasant and the farmer, but he actually lived like a villager. To assert that "All that is good and wise is Western, and all that is evil and foolish is Eastern or Indian," would be adopting a complacency which would harm the cause of democracy and create more misunderstandings.

My visit to the West has been most enlightening and revealing. It is my honest opinion that the Western world is badly in need of knowing what India really is and what it actually stands for. I find that the scanty information available to the average man in the Western world is often highly prejudicial, distorted and most damaging. If a little knowledge is a dangerous thing, distorted knowledge is disastrous. If I want to know the import of Western culture the two ways open to me are either to live in the West and observe it personally or to get to know it from Western writers. But in adopting the second way, however dispassionate a foreigner may be he cannot cast off his pre-occupation of mind and give a true account of the culture of another country, unless he also adopts the first way and has lived in that country and learned about it from the original works in the native language through the native scholars. The same attitude is necessary for knowing the facts about India. It is with the idea of clarifying certain prevalent misunderstandings that I have undertaken to state certain facts with reference to the political development of India, particularly after the partition. I will therefore describe both the good and the bad, the ugly and the laudable aspects of the development of democracy in my country.

I have stated that Gandhi lifted the masses of India and mobilized them for peaceful revolution during India's struggle for independence. He was not blind to the backwardness and illiteracy among the villagers who formed the bulk of Indian population. He had even suggested that the task of uplifting the villagers was more urgent and more important than the attainment of independence. He had launched a movement called "Gram Sudhar," or village uplift, and carried it out most enthusiastically. Had he not done so the villagers, most of whom were peasants and manual workers, tenants and underlings of big landlords would have fallen easy prey to Communist propaganda. He was a farsighted politician and a most pragmatic political thinker. He prepared the nation not only for handling the national government successfully, but also prepared her to fight the potential totalitarian threat to the freedom of India. He knew that the key to the success of democracy in India lay in improving the lot of the villages through evolution as opposed to revolution. In order to do that he urged that the urban people share the joys and sorrows of the rural people and help the villagers to develop and improve socially, economically and politically. An American writer has quoted Gandhi in this context and has written: "Gandhi urged the city people to go to the villages and there come in 'living touch with the poor by working for them in their midst, sharing their sorrows, understanding their difficulties, anticipating their wants.' He contended that, 'whether the British remain or not, it is our duty always to wipe out unemployment, to bridge the gulf between rich and poor, to banish communal strife, to exorcise the demon of untouchability— If crores (millions) of people do not take a living interest in this nation-building work, freedom must remain a dream and unattainable either by violence or nonviolence.' He enjoined the ancient Hindu principle of trusteeship on the big landlords, the princes, and other rich people, reminding them that wealth is only to share with and serve the interests of the poor."

This was in fact the manifesto which the Congress Party adopted after it captured political power, and the progress of democracy in India has largely been the result of acting on this will of Gandhi. It would be an exaggeration to say that all the social, economic and political problems of India have been solved—by no means. But the attempt to solve these problems democratically is commendable, because it shows gradual progress towards democratic goals and the destination of the demand of equality—social, political and economic. Gandhi feared disaster if these problems were not solved democratically. But luckily they have been tackled in the manner Gandhi wished and this method is yielding good results. That is why I say that Gandhi could foresee the totalitarian danger to Indian democracy and that he forewarned his countrymen by preparing them for evolution to save them from violent revolution. Who can deny the magnificent achievement on the part of the Congress government in successfully persuading the ruling princes to abdicate their thrones and to turn over the right of the government to the farmer and the peasant? Was it not the execution of the idea of "trusteeship" advocated by Gandhi? The same principle was followed by various state governments while abolishing feudalism and landlordship, thereby distributing the land among the landless tillers. Two big states of India, Uttar Pradesh and Rajasthan, which were the centers of the old system of feudalism fostered by the British and the princely rulers, demonstrated the truth of "trusteeship" by abolishing landlordship and feudalism democratically and nonviolently through legislation and adequate compensation. The other states also followed them and brought about land reforms. This was the most important perceptible progress made by Indian democracy.

During British rule the tenants were in the constant awe and fear of the landlord or the feudal chief. In princely states the feudal lords got forced labor from the poor and innocent peasants. Getting forced labor was supposed to be the right of the feudal lords. With the adoption of democracy all these evils ended virtually immediately, and for the first time the ignorant villager realized that forced labor was slavery. Besides the disappearance of social injustice, the introduction of an unconditional franchise and the successful conduct of the first general election in 1952 gave a sense of importance and self-respect to the downtrodden villagers. It was really astonishing even for educated Indians and the political leaders to note the fervor and the enthusiasm with which these hundreds of millions of illiterate voters participated in the first general election throughout the length and breadth of the vast country. When I refer to the successful conduct of the three general elections of India in spite of the prevalent illiteracy, Western listeners often doubt the truth of the statement. They cannot (rightly, to a great extent) imagine that an illiterate person is capable of exercising the right to vote, much less to win an election. But it is true that India has gone through three general elections successfully and that most of the candidates have been elected on personal merit. What puzzles a Westerner is how an illiterate can register his vote without any education whatsoever.

This curiosity on the part of Westerners is natural. I would therefore like to explain the method of election which India evolved to insure maximum secrecy of voting by ballot and to educate the illiterate voter beforehand to insure that he votes for the men whom he wants elected. Much training had to be given to voters before launching the general elections, and this training was also tested in many local elections of municipal boards, etc., before the finalization of the technique to be adopted at the general elections. In should prove interesting for readers to know how the election department of the government of India gained experience through observation and how it gradually improved the method of voting suited to the illiterate electorate.

Prior to the attainment of independence, when a minimum economic standard or literacy was the prerequisite for the right to vote, municipal elections used to be held all over India. But the number of voters was limited owing to the above-mentioned restrictions, and for the most part the literate voters exercised their right to vote by putting a cross or "X" against the name of the candidate on the ballot. But now that all the restrictions of literacy and minimum income were removed it was necessary to invent some simple way of making the voter understand the differences between candidates. Mere printing of the names of the candidates would be meaningless to the illiterate voter. Therefore at the time of municipal elections, before the general elections were held, the method of introducing symbols along with the names of the candidates on the ballot paper was introduced. The idea was to observe how the unconditional adult franchise would work. Observations made at these elections helped the Election Commission of India to improve the method of recording votes to insure maximum efficiency in the conduct of general elections. Before I explain the method of election which was adopted at the first and the second general elections I would like to mention the various handicaps experienced at the earlier municipal elections.

After the attainment of independence the municipal elections were considerably different from such elections held prior to independence. The method of recording a vote was to put a cross against the symbol of the candidate whom the voter chose. Suppose there were three candidates, A, B and C. A was given the symbol "cycle", B was given "cow", and C was given "elephant." The voters had to go inside the polling booth, get a ballot paper from the presiding officer, retire to a polling compartment covered with a screen, put the cross mark against the symbol, say, "cycle", or "cow", come out of the compartment with the folded ballot paper, and insert the marked ballot paper in the one ballot box lying before the presiding officer. The box was, of course, sealed just before the start of the poll in the presence of the candidates or their agents. Only a slit was left open for inserting the ballot papers. It was a simple method. But since for the first time the entire adult population had to vote the election officers faced many problems. The rush of the voters was unexpected and it was felt that a larger number of polling booths was desirable. Similarly there were other experiences which resulted in many innovations introduced into the general elections. One particular incident is interesting as well as illuminating. At one polling station meant only for women voters my wife was the presiding officer. During the time of polling one lady who had been fully instructed by the supporter of the candidate with the symbol "cow" came to record her vote. She had been instructed to be very particular and cautious in putting the cross mark on "cow", meaning thereby the symbol, or, rather, the picture of the cow on the ballot. When this lady entered the polling station she was given the ballot paper and a pencil. She said "Where is the cow? I have to put the cross mark on the cow and nowhere else." The presiding officer said, "Dear lady, we have given you the ballot paper. It contains all the symbols including the cow. Please go inside that compartment and put a cross mark with the pencil against any of these symbols you like." The woman replied "No! No! I will not be deceived by you. I was told that people will mislead me. I am not going to be duped by you. Show me the cow! cow! cow! I will put the cross mark only on the cow and nothing else!"

No amount of argument could convince this illiterate but adamant voter to follow the procedure for voting mentioned by the presiding officer. This event was recorded in the report. Many such difficulties were reported. After the ballot papers were counted it was noted that many voters had left the ballot paper blank. Some had put the cross on the wrong side and some on the symbol itself. Therefore a simpler method of recording votes was adopted in the first general election. According to that procedure the names and the symbols of the candidates were not put on the ballot paper. On the contrary, each candidate was allotted a separate ballot box with his symbol affixed thereto. These ballot boxes were specially prepared. The presiding officer had to seal the boxes in the presence of the candidates or their agents before polling started. These boxes were placed in a compartment covered with a screen. The presiding officer along with the other polling officers would sit just outside this compartment in the polling station. As a voter came to record his vote at the entrance to the station he would meet a polling officer with a list of voters. After getting the serial number of his name from this first polling officer, he entered the polling station and came to the second polling officer having a similar list and a bundle of printed ballots, the account of which would be strictly maintained. The voter handed over the slip containing his serial number to the second polling officer who in turn announced the name, parentage, and the age of the voter aloud so that the candidates or their agents present in the room might hear it. The purpose of this announcement was to insure that the voter was certified. If there was any doubt about his identity the candidates or his agents would have the right to challenge his vote. In case of a challenge there would be a different procedure to record the vote and to leave room for futher legal proceedings after the election. Normally, when the voter's name was announced and there was no challenge with regard to his identity, he would get a ballot from the second polling officer and proceed towards the polling compartment. But before voting the third polling officer would put a mark of indelible ink on the back of the second finger of his left hand to prevent "repeaters". The voter would enter the compartment, and after viewing all the symbols on the boxes, drop his ballot in the box of the candidate of his choice. This procedure was adopted during the first two elections and it worked well. But during the third election the procedure was altered yet again. It was now felt that the procedure of putting the cross mark against the name and symbol of the candidate on the printed ballot paper could be reintroduced in view of the experience gained by the electorate in the two previous general elections. So in the general election of 1962 the voters were required to put a cross mark on the ballot paper by means of a rubber stamp bearing the cross mark. However the cross mark could be put anywhere on the line on which the name and symbol of the candidate was printed. This procedure was successful during the third general election in India.

The description given above indicates the progress of democracy at work in India. Introducing the democratic method of election in a huge electorate of two hundred million voters is a herculean task. The conduct of elections is not only costly but very delicate. The officers appointed as presiding and polling officers have a great responsibility in conducting the election peacefully, justly, and carefully. It requires a good deal of patience, toleration and discretion to conduct elections in the villages successfully. The voters are very enthusiastic and are at times fanatic in voting for and supporting the candidate of their choice. There is sometimes the danger of rioting and disturbance in the village where there is keen competition and tension during election days. The majority of the village folk are a simple unassuming people who can be won with love. They want to vote for the candidate of their choice and are also amenable to provocation. There are bound to be misunderstandings and misrepresentations created by the contesting parties. But if the election officers are honest, intelligent and sincere, they enjoy the work. I feel that conducting elections in India is a nation-building work and a real service to the illiterate masses of the country. I would like to elaborate this point with reference to my personal experience during the third general election of 1962.

I was appointed presiding officer of a polling party consisting of myself, six polling officers and three unarmed police constables, one of whom was a head constable. We had to conduct the election at three polling stations in three different villages on different dates. We were provided with a bus and started for our first polling station two days earlier than the actual date of the poll. It was a long journey over a rough and rugged road to the interior of the rural area. We reached the village late in the afternoon and were received by the school teacher and the village official, accompanied by a few villagers who were to assist us. They were like us all non-party men. The election was to be held in a small building of the local school and the polling party had also to remain in the building for two nights. It was winter and the nights were terribly cold. We were provided with only three rough cots and most of us had to spread our beds on the hard ground. There was no electricity in the village and we had to light a kerosene lamp which we had brought with us. We had two kerosene stoves of our own and we cooked meals ourselves. The room in which we slept opened in the compound of the school and had no shutters on the doors. There was no heating system. Our quilts and blankets were the only protection against the cold. Since we were exhausted on account of the long journey we slept well in spite of the severe cold.

Next morning we got busy setting up the polling station. All the polling officers cooperated with zeal. Many villagers, particularly the leading persons, the merchants, the elected members of the local assembly, called Panchayat, and the village revenue officer came to meet us and volunteered assistance required for the successful conduct of the election. In the evening one young man, the only highly educated man in the village, a college graduate, came to me and wanted to talk to me privately. He appeared puzzled and panicky, but was no doubt seriously concerned about the conduct of the election. He was actively supporting one of the two candidates and had been canvassing for his own party for several months. The areas of the constituency covered by our polling station was quite wide and included three villages, two of which were situated at a distance of three to five miles from the polling station. This young man had just returned from his election campaign from the other two villages and was perhaps harassed by the supporters of the opposite party. Obviously there was a considerable tension in that area and the authorities were quite conscious of it. Mr. Madan Lal was the name of the young man. He perhaps knew me as a professor of the college which he had attended (though not as a student of mine) and he said to me, "Sir, I want to know how many armed policemen have you brought with you?" I was a bit surprised at the question and asked him, "Mr. Madan Lal, why are you worrying about armed policemen? I don't need any protection."

Madan Lal: Sir, you don't know. This is the area populated by fierce Rajputs. They are all armed. A majority of them are supporting the anti-Congress candidate and are deadly against the government.

Myself: Dear Madan Lal, do you know that a government servant has nothing to do with any political party? Congress party may be in power by virtue of the previous election, but I have nothing to do with that. I am here as the servant of my nation and my duty is to see that the election is held impartially and that every voter freely exercises his franchise.

Madan Lal: Sir, I understand this. But the Rajputs who may shoot their neighbor on a simple provocation, are mostly illiterate, and they might create some trouble tomorrow. There is a great tension in the whole area.

Myself: I do not bother about the tension. I am sure that there cannot be any disturbance.

Madan Lal: But how many armed policemen have you brought with you?

Myself: I have only three unarmed policemen.

Madan Lal: Sir, you are a philosopher and election is something real—a real battle. I am warning you that there is a great tension here and some violence, even firing is likely to happen tomorrow. You had better summon armed police for your assistance tomorrow.

I was not at all disturbed because I knew that I could convince the villagers of the importance of an impartial and peaceful election and could impress upon them the evils of quarrels and fights which would undermine the spirit of democracy. So I sent the young man away with assurance that all would go well the next day. He was not convinced, however, and still expected violence. Later in the evening an armed police party came to our village on patrol duty, and the commander wanted to know whether I required his assistance next day. Obviously the District Magistrate, who was also the Returns Officer of the district, had sensed tension in that area and had instructed the police to be vigilant in the maintenance of law and order. I refused any assistance from the armed police and said to the commander of the party that I would cope with the situation myself.

However, I called the two leading elected members of the local assembly (Panchayat), who belonged to the two contending parties, to give them some instructions. Both of them were very courteous and sensible. They agreed to instruct their voters to maintain law and order. I told them that no canvassing should be done within one hundred yards of the polling station by either party. Though they were illiterate and were perhaps bitter enemies, I found that they were amenable to reason. I said to both of them that the purpose of election was to elect a suitable representative of the constituency who should help the community to develop, and that election was a constructive step towards nation-building. Hence mutual bitterness and rifts would undermine the very purpose of election. I told them that both the candidates belonged to a place outside the area covered by that polling station and that one of them was to be elected. Since either of the candidates would be an outsider, it would be foolish for the villagers to resort to quarrels for the sake of an outsider and to have a permanent rift in the village community thereby undermining its social, economic, and political development. I therefore suggested to them that all the villagers shake off their personal prejudices and adopt an impersonal attitude while voting. To my amazement the suggestion had a wonderful effect. The two local leaders embraced each other in my presence as two brothers. Both of them went to address the villagers and communicated what I had expressed. On the next day the election was most peaceful. The villagers, men, women, young and old came in queue and quietly voted for the candidate of their own choice. They were all quite satisfied. Over sixty percent of the eligible votes were cast. When our party was about to leave a crowd of villagers thronged to give us a warm farewell. They watched us loading the bus and expressed their gratitude on the peaceful conclusion of the polling. Some veterans of the village came to me and said that they were obliged for my valuable advice of bridging the mutual differences for the development of the community and of being impersonal while voting. The villagers waved to us and expressed sorrow on our departure as if they were separating from their kith and kin. This experience and feeling were shared by all the members of the polling party. I felt that real India lives in the villages and that the rural people only need proper guidance and sympathetic advice.

CHAPTER VI

Democracy and Economic Progress*

The progress of democracy in India, which has stimulated political consciousness throughout the length and breadth of the country, is closely linked with its economic progress. Since the British government paid little or no attention to India's economic progress and the technological development of the country, democracy made little headway. Of course it could also be put another way: Britain had no interest in the growth of democracy in India. In fact, as has been shown in this book, she resolutely opposed it, being far more interested in tapping India's wealth than in providing India with the training and the conditions which would lead to political consciousness and self-government. It is often difficult to separate sharply one set of facts (the political, say) from another set (the economic) in this tangled area of causes and effects, but that British interests were mainly economic and that her interests in political matters in India were chiefly to keep Indians in a state of political innocence and subjugation—these facts are well-documented.

Before any attempt is made to review the economic efforts and achievements of India and its relation to the faith of Indians in democracy as opposed to communism, it may be worthwhile to state that the millions of illiterate Indians who until recently were thought of as unfit for self-government by foreign rulers have proved by their active participation in national plans that illiteracy

---

*Debnath Mookherjee, co-author of this chapter, is on the faculty of Western Washington State College at Bellingham, Washington. He received his M.Sc. degree from the University of Calcutta and Ph.D. from the University of Florida.

is no handicap in making democracy a success and in developing the economy of the villages. The adoption of what is known as "democratic decentralization" in India is a successful experiment which has brought freedom to the door of every villager. The adoption of this democratic system, also called the "panchayat raj", or government of the elected five-membered village assembly, is in fact democracy in action among the teeming millions of the country. It has both advantages and disadvantages. But it is no doubt a great politico-economic experiment which has changed and is going to change further the face of India. It is believed that the greater the success attained by the adoption of this system, the greater are the chances of survival of democracy in India (in spite of the danger of a thrust of communism on its borders) as it seeks to entrust the people with the function of control, initiation and implemention of ideas directly related to their lives. It may, therefore, be quite relevant to discuss this development of Indian democracy in some detail.

Democracy must be flexible in its structure and constitution in different countries according to the social, political and economic atmosphere prevailing in them. This does not necessarily mean that democracy is of various kinds. On the contrary, democracy is a general term which has the specific meaning of being a representative "government of the people, by the people and for the people", as opposed to totalitarianism, which is a government opposed to freedom and representation. It is only with reference to the details of the constitution and the different conditions or levels at which representative government is introduced in various countries that democracies vary. Indian politicians think that the greater the decentralization, the wider the scope and range of democracy. This is what is meant by individual freedom, the protection of which is the prime object of democracy. The unit of democracy is the individual, because it is the individual who votes in a government; but countries and states are also units, as it is through these institutions that the will of the individual is executed. In a vast country like India, these larger units (larger than individuals) have very great importance particularly because of the cultural and economic background of this country. In India the family has traditionally been the social unit, and next to the family the caste. But most of the people still depend on farming and live in villages. On account of this agro-economic structure of Indian society, the political and

economic unit in the country has been and will be for the for-
seeable future the village, or "gram" as it is called in Hindi. That
is why Gandhi and Tagore always laid stress on the uplift of the
villages or "gram sudhar", which literally means "village reforma-
tion".

A study of this aspect of Indian democracy is most important
because this is the special feature which distinguishes India from
the highly developed industrial democracies like America, on the
one hand, and radical totalitarian communistic countries like Red
China, on the other. The village panchayat, or elected assembly,
cannot be called a commune, though it is a community in the general American sense of the term. In India there is a state legislature
and state ministry in every individual state. The state is further
split up into smaller units of elected bodies called district councils.
The "zila parishad" or district council may be compared to the
county council in America. But the comparison here would be in-
complete because these district councils in India are the representatives of the smaller units called "panchayat samitis," or village
assembly associations. These village assembly associations are the
representative bodies of the smallest units called "gram panchayats",
or village assemblies, which are directly elected by each and every
village. The villages are usually very small, often with a population
of one hundred or less, and generally consist of peasants and
farmers. This is how democracy in India has literally reached every
adult citizen both from the point of view of legislation and administration.

As long as India was under British rule a feudal system prevailed everywhere and the peasants and farmers who worked from
morning until evening in the fields were exploited. The landlord
or feudal lord, who seldom visited his farms, received the entire
profit from the crops, and the field worker could not earn even
two square meals a day for his family. The landlord was honored
by his tenants who were virtually his slaves. They arranged for the
hunt, or shikar, served him with the best possible meals they could
procure, and attended him throughout this stay in the village. He
was really the overlord. He talked to them as a master would talk
to his slave, a ruler to the ruled. The imperial government depended
on him for the collection of revenue from the tenants and sub-
landlords, and he was usually honored with a title from the British
government. Minor disputes between villagers were to be settled

by him. He was the administrator, executive, collector, and sometimes also the judge of the few villages which constituted his landed
territory. Although the panchayat, an assembly of five elected chiefs,
existed at that time, this body had mainly social jurisdiction and
passed moral judgments in case of any misbehavior of some villager
whose conduct came into conflict with the traditional morality. At
its beginning this panchayat was a political unit, but when feudalism predominated it became merely a social institution. The landlord became more important than the panchayat due to his economic and political status. The disputes of property-owners were
decided by the courts, and litigation was a great curse. The poor
farmers who owned small holdings were often ruined when they
fell victim to litigation. Moreover the farmer usually ran into debt
as a result of crop-failure when the rains failed. He had to borrow
money for buying bullocks and ploughs for farming. Most of the
time he would mortgage his land and ultimately sell it out to the
money lender at a low price and become his serf to earn his liveli-
hood. These were the conditions of the villages in India prior to
the attainment of independence. Of course such conditions are
conducive for the advent of communism, which thrives on hunger,
want and injustice, along with economic, social and political in-
equality. But all these challenges were met in India by the introduction of democratic decentralization. Without land reform and
the introduction of a completely democratic system of government,
which gave the responsibility of administration to every voter, these
evils probably could not have been effectively dealt with to avoid
communism.

The panchayat is therefore the key political unit of the country.
All adult members of the village community elect the panchayat
by secret ballot throughout the states. From the five elected members
of the panchayat, a "sarpanch" or leader is elected. This elected
body is not only entrusted with the function of control, but also
with the matters related to furthering an all-round development
of the village community. Village sanitation and improvement of
public health facilities are the "obligatory" functions of the
panchayat. In addition, it is concerned with such activities as
providing improved seeds and fertilizers to the farmers, supplying
irrigation water, arranging loans from co-operative banks for buying agricultural equipment, promoting cottage industry and educational facilities, etc. What the panchayat raj seeks is to create

an atmosphere in village India so that the people can express themselves on the matters of administrative, social, and economic life of the country.

Some people criticize the introduction of this panchayat system and blame the presently ruling Congress Party. The opposition parties sometimes say that under the garb of giving local self-government to the villages and by giving financial aid to the panchayats, the party wants to win the favor of the electorate and sweep the general elections. However, this view is not shared by a majority of the people.

In spite of the venture on the part of the people of India to make democracy a success, it has to be admitted that povery has always been and will be a major breeding ground of communism, and there is no denying the fact that both political and economic progress are interrelated and interdependent. On the other hand, not only some concrete material achievement but a dynamic attempt for a betterment of conditions has a long range value for the morale of the people to fight off communism. The question, therefore, is what efforts towards progress has India made after the attainment of freedom so far as its economic aspect is concerned? The answer to this question would also be helpful in seeking an answer to the basic question, why India has not gone Red.

After independence the government of India embarked on a policy of planned economy. A planning commission was set up in March 1950, to provide the plans for improvement in the living standards of the people through the "most effective and balanced utilization of the country's resources." Under the Colonial rule of Great Britain, India had no significant industrial base and no attempt was made to utilize the vast natural resources of the country. Most of the people were dependent on an agricultural economy, but the methods of production were primitive, the peasants relied too much on the uncertain monsoon and in some areas famine was an annual event. No new innovations or modern techniques of production were known to the cultivators, nor did they have the opportunities to better their knowledge through education. India remained underdeveloped. So, after independence, in order to mitigate these problems, a Five Year Plan system was initiated "aiming not merely at the development of resources" but also at the development of "human faculties and the building up of an institutional framework adequate to the needs and aspirations of people." [1]

Indian planning is a unique experiment because a successful combination of democracy and planning is indeed a rarity.[2] Unlike China, Indian planning is not based on totalitarian methods but upon democratic procedures. Free and open discussion, notwithstanding its imminent disadvantage of being somewhat slow, controversial and open to public criticism, has been a distinctive and proud feature of Indian planning. The planning commission of India is an 'economic' rather than a 'political' organ of the government. Planning at the state level is carried on by the departments of development and planning of the individual states. The Central Planning Commission co-operates with states in the matter of formulation and implementation of plan proposals. There are various co-ordinating committees to assist in the planning work both at the state and below the state level, as in districts, blocks or villages.

India exhibits a great deal of change in the nature of her economy since the adoption of Five Year Planning. The Indian economy is a mixed one which contains elements of both socialism and capitalism. The private sector contributes a large share of total investment—here individuals or groups undertake business in such enterprises as in agricultural productions, consumer goods industries like textiles, sugar, matches, oil, soap, etc. The film industry in India is considered one of the best in the world and is entirely a private enterprise. The State or Public sector has assumed the responsibility of developing certain heavy industries such as steel and metallurgy, heavy chemicals, etc., and the locomotive industry, communications (excluding a major part of road transport), life insurance (excluding general insurance) and the aircraft industry are also under direct control of the government. However, certain pre-existing heavy industry, e.g., Tata Iron and Steel, was allowed to remain in the private sector. The role of the public sector in the development of an underdeveloped country like India should not be underestimated. The private sector is primarily concerned with

[1]*India: Some Facts* (Information Service of India, Embassy of India, Washington 8, D. C. U.S.A.) p. 56.
[2]C. L. Khanna, "Perspective of India's Planned Progress and Prosperity", *The Modern Review,* p. 179, March, 1964 (Calcutta, India).

profit-making enterprises, and the interests of the common man may never be the concern of the private sector.[3] The basic objective of economic planning of India is to secure equitable distribution of human and material resources—and it can best be done through private initiative and enterprise supplemented by governmental planning, advice and assistance. It is noteworthy, that the government is encouraging individual enterprise and granting liberal loans and subsidies to those who want to start new industries.

During the last fifteen years, through the three Five-Year plans, India has attempted to move from a basically agrarian economy to an agro-industrial one. The plans emphasized the detailed program of development of agriculture, industry, trade, power, transport and social services. In the scheduled Fourth Five-Year plan to be completed in 1970 these goals have been extended to foster further economic and social progress and self-reliance.

Being an economically underdeveloped country under foreign rule for centuries, India had developed and fostered a multitude of problems, the principal ones of which may be specified in the areas of agriculture, industry and the education of its ever increasing population. In spite of its many failures, disappointments, and possible planning errors, independent India has mostly been successful in her effort to control the intensity of almost all of these problems, which may be accounted for as one of the major factors in the reaffirmation of the faith of her citizens in the values of democracy.

Improper fertilization, poor seed quality, lack of scientific and modern ways or techniques of cultivation, subdivision and fragmentation of land, and uncertainty of water supply as a result of insufficient irrigation, all these factors and others as well were responsible in varying degrees for intensifying the agricultural problems of India. All three Five-Year plans have emphasized the need to rectify these problems and some of the achievements through planning are shown in Table I. A number of fertilizer factories have been established in India and the consumption and availability of different kinds of fertilizers are more and more appreciated by the farmers. Approximately 120 million acres of land have come under improved seeds in place of the 4.7 million acres in 1955-56.

[3]P. Chakravarti, "The Nature and Problems of a Mixed Economy", *The Calcutta Review*, p. 114, August, 1965 (Calcutta, India).

TABLE 1

PATTERNS OF PROGRESS IN PLANNING: AGRICULTURE, IRRIGATION AND POWER

	Unit	1950-51	1955-56 (End of 1st Plan)	% Inc.	1960-61 (End of 2nd Plan)	% Inc.	1965-66 (End of 3rd Plan)	% Inc.	1970-71 (End of 4th Plan)	% Inc.
AGRICULTURE PRODUCTION										
Index. No. of Agricultural P.	1949-50 = 100	95.6	116.8	22.18	142.2	21.76	158.3	11.32	207.8	31.3
Food Grains Production	M tons	54.92	69.22	26.64	82.02	18.49	72.29	−11.8	120	33.3
Cotton	M bales	2.62	4.03	53.82	5.29	31.27	4.73	−10.59	8.6	81.8
Sugarcane	M tons	6.92	7.29	5.33	11.2	53.64	12.12	8.21	13.5	11.4
Oilseeds	M tons	5.09	5.63	10.61	6.98	23.93	6.14	12.04	10.7	74.3
Jute	M bales	3.51	4.48	27.64	4.13	−7.81	4.48	8.47	9.0	100.9
Tea	Th. tons	273	285	4.40	321	12.63	376	17.19	475	
Tobacco	Th. tons	261	303	10.09	307	1.32	400	30.29		18.7
Fish	M tons	.7	1.0	42.86	1.4	40.00	1.15	−17.86	1.53	83.0
Milk	M tons	17.0	19.0	11.76	22.0	15.79	24.6	11.82	32.25	31.1
Wool	M lbs.	60.0	65.0	8.83	72.0	10.77	83.0	18.28	94.0	13.2
AGRICULTURAL SERVICES										
Minor irrigation (a)	M acres		9.5		9.0	−5.26	13.1	45.56	17.0	29.8
Land Reclamation (a)	M acres		2.8		2.3	−17.86	4.2	82.61	2.5	
Soil Conservation (a)	M acres		.7		2.5	257.14	9.8	292.00	20.0	104.1
Nitrogenous Fertilizers (c)	Th. tons of N	56	107	91.07	210	96.26	600	185.71	2,000	233.3
Phosphatic Fertilizer (c)	Th. tons of P205	7	13	83.71	70	438.46	150	114.29	1,000	568.7
Potassic Fertilizer (c)	Th. tons of K20	6	12	100.00	26	110.67	90	240.18	1,350	288.8
Organic and Green Manures										
a. Urban compost	M tons		2.15		3.05	41.57	3.4	11.48	5.4	63.2
b. Green manures	M acres				11.8		21.5	82.20	64.0	151.2
Plant protection	M acres				16.0		41.0	156.25	137.0	234.1
Area under improved seeds	M acres		4.7		55.0	1170.21	120.0	118.18	274.0	128.8
IRRIGATION AND POWER										
Major and medium irrigation (a)										
a. Potential at channel outlets	M acres		6.5		5.2	−20.00	6.3	21.15	13.0	102.3
b. Utilization	M acres		3.1		5.2	67.74	5.5	5.77	9.0	63.6
Power										
a. Electricity: installed cap.	M KW	2.3	3.4	47.83	5.6	64.71	10.2	82.14	20.0	88.1
b. Electricity generated	M KWH	6,575	10,777	63.91	24.209	124.64	36,400	50.36	80,000	119.8
c. Towns/villages electrified	Thousands	3.7	7.4	100.00	24.2	227.02	52.3	116.12	110.0	110.3
d. Pumps energized	Millions				1.6		4.8	200.00	11.8	145.8
PER CAPITA LEVEL										
Food grains	Ozs. per capita per day	13.9	15.2	9.35	16.4	7.89	15.4	−0.10	18.1	17.8

SOURCE: *Weekly India News*, September 23, 1966. Information Service of India, Embassy of India, Washington, D. C.
(a) additional, (c) consumed, M—Million, Th.—Thousand, cap.—capacity, P—Production.

The village panchayates have taken keen interest in the distribution of the fertilizers and seeds. The knowledge of modern techniques and ways of cultivation are brought to the farmers mostly by the Community Development workers, and mechanized farming is being gradually introduced. The village panchayates and co-operatives have started supplying tractors on rent to the peasants and the system is gaining ground. The government, on its part, extends loans and subsidies to cultivators for the purchase of agricultural equipment. The problems associated with subdivision and fragmentation of land have been controlled by land reform laws in almost all states of India. Acquisition of land from the absentee landlords on payment of a reasonable compensation, or their voluntary donation of land for cultivation by the landless tillers has helped the government to provide fine land for the farmers. Along with these land reform attempts, a movement to eliminate the disparity in the ownership of agricultural land (Bhudan Movement) has been launched by Acharya Vinova Bhave, a staunch disciple of Mahatma Gandhi. The philosophy he propounded is called "Sarvodaya", which aims at the all-round development of all persons without distinction of caste, creed and sex. He has rallied around him hundreds of workers recruited from all walks of life and all classes of society devoted to the task of obtaining voluntary gifts of land from the big landowners and distributing it among the landless cultivators. The significance of this movement lies not so much in its achievement as in the spirit behind it which gives the observer an idea how India is fighting against Communism both ideologically and pragmatically.

In order to utilize the vast tracts of land uncultivated for lack of water supply major emphasis has been given to irrigation. As a result, various irrigation projects and multipurpose projects have been initiated in almost all the states of India and efforts are being made to supply water (and electricity) to every village. It is a stupendous task and needs time to be properly carried out. But the progress in this respect has led villagers to hope that water shortages even in dry areas might be terminated in the near future. In spite of controversy among the critics regarding its practicability, this optimism may have a special value for the faith of the people in democratic planning.

Along with agriculture, development of industry has been a major concern of the planners of India. Although the country is endowed with vast natural resources such as coal, iron ore, mica, manganese, and bauxite, little attention was paid in the past to proper utilization of these resources. India has high potentialities of hydro power development. Along with these, manpower, if properly utilized, can make India an industrial giant in future years. The most notable achievements in the industrial development programs have been the expansion and diversification of the basic capital and producer goods industries—steel, cement, transport, machine tools, etc. Table 2 shows the development of selected industries since 1951 and the fourth Five-Year plan targets. Though relatively more emphasis is placed on the development of heavy industries, special attention has been given to the revival and improvement of India's traditional cottage industries, because it provides an effective means of reducing unemployment and brings stability in the economy of rural India.

However, not only the natural resources in the country, but also the technical knowledge to utilize them properly is an essential factor in the developmental process. In the technological and scientific field, India is probably next only to United States and Soviet Union in the number of engineering and technology students she produces. Scores of new universities and technological schools and colleges have been established and higher research in science and technology is encouraged in many ways. Besides the Ministry of Education in the government there is a special ministry for scientific research, and thousands of capable students receive scholarships and financial aid for higher studies in science and technology at home and abroad. Indian scientists working in the government Atomic Research Institute can produce nuclear weapons. In spite of these developments as shown in Table 3, in proportion to her population India is still short of technologists, scientists and medical doctors. It is again noteworthy that medical aid in India is free for all. Not only medicine but even surgery of every kind is free in the hospitals run by the government and staffed by highly qualified and efficient surgeons and physicians. These facilities are not only provided in large cities but even the rural population can avail themselves of them. There are government dispensaries within the reach of the villagers in almost every state. Mobile medical and surgical units tour the villages and conduct free medical operations and treatment. It was only after independence that such facilities were made available to the villagers

TABLE 2

PATTERNS OF PROGRESS IN PLANNING: INDUSTRY, MINERAL, TRANSPORT AND COMMUNICATION

	Unit	1950-51	1955-56 (End of 1st Plan)	% Inc.	1960-61 (End of 2nd Plan)	% Inc.	1965-66 (End of 3rd Plan)	% Inc.	1970-71 (End of 4th Plan)	% Inc.
INDUSTRIAL PRODUCTION										
Index numbers of industrial p.	1956 = 100	73.5	91.9		130.1	41.59	181.6	39.58	306.0	63.5
Steel ingots	M tons	1.47	1.74	18.37	3.4	96.40	6.2	82.35	11.7	88.7
Finished steel	M tons	1.04	1.3	25.00	2.3	76.92	4.6	100.00	8.8	91.3
Aluminum	Th. tons	4	7.4	75.00	18.3	171.42	65	242.10	330	407.7
Machine tools (graded)	Rs. Ms.	3	8	168.67	70	773.00	230	228.67	1,050	365.5
Sulphuric acid	Th. tons	101	167	63.63	361	121.34	664	82.92	2,400	261.4
Petroleum products	M tons	.2	3.4	1600.00	5.8	70.59	9.8	70.65	20.0	102.0
Mill-made cloth	M meters	3,401	4,665	37.17	4,649	-0.33	4,434	-4.63	5,486	23.7
Handloom, powerloom and khadi cloth	M meters	917	1,643	79.17	2,072	26.11	3,146	51.83	4,572	45.3
Total cloth production	M meters	4,318	6,308	48.09	6,721	6.55	7,580	12.87	10,058	32.7
Industrial estates	Numbers		1		66	6500.00	300	54.64	550	83.3
MINERALS										
Iron ore	M tons	3	4.3	43.33	11.0	155.81	23.0	109.09	54.0	134.3
Coal	M tons	32.8	39.0	18.90	55.7	42.32	70.0	25.67	106.0	51.4
TRANSPORT SERVICES										
Railways										
a. Passenger kilometers	Hundred M	66.5	62.4	-6.17	77.7	24.52	96.0	23.58	119.0	24.0
b. Freight carried	M tons	93	116	24.73	156	34.49	205	23.90	308	50.2
Road surfaced	Th. k-meters	156	183	17.31	235	28.40	284	17.19	334	17.6
Shipping	Million Grt.	.39	.48	23.07	.86	79.16	1.54	79.06	3.0	94.8
Commercial vehicles on road	Thousands	116.3	165.6	43.10	224.0	12.68	320.0	52.33	525.0	64.9
Major ports: Traffic handled	M tons	19.3	23.4	21.24	38.8	65.81	50.2	29.88	82.5	64.2
COMMUNICATIONS										
Post offices	Thousands	36	55	52.78	77	40.00	98	27.27	110	12.2
Telegraph offices	Thousands	3.6	5.1	41.67	6.9	35.29	8.7	26.09	10.6	21.8
Telephones	Thousands	168	278	65.43	463	68.58	873	88.55	1,523	74.4
Cloth	Meters per capita per annum	8.4	14.2	69.05	14.2		14.9	4.82	16.9	13.4

SOURCE: *Weekly India News*, September 23, 1966. Information Service of India, Embassy of India, Washington, D. C. M—Million, Th.—Thousand, p—production.

and that the mobile medical and surgical units were fostered in many states. These are the advantages of democracy and freedom for the illiterate, teeming millions of India.

In spite of all the material achievements during the last one and a half decade of planning, the level of the standard of living of the Indian people has not gone up correspondingly, primarily due to the great increase of population. India is the second most populous country with an estimated total of 498 million people in 1965-66, greater than that of the United States and Soviet Union combined. The population is rising at a rate of 2.2 per cent a year and this enormous increase has been one of the greatest obstacles in the efforts at raising the standard of living. The growth patterns of the national income and population since 1950 are shown in Table 4. The national income is rising but the higher rate of population growth overshadows the gains of planning. This problem is very much alive to the minds of Indian planners and India has taken up family planning as a national program and encouraging results are emerging, however slowly. In the Fourth plan special provisions of mass education, training, services and research have been made to accelerate the progress of the plan for controlling the population explosion. Recently, a Family Planning department has been created in the Ministry of Health and six regional family planning offices have been set up for review of policies and effective communication with the states regarding policy matters. A Family Welfare Program Center for every 50,000 population has been proposed to facilitate the availability of contraceptives and services related to sterilization. It is significant to note that the total number of sterilizations performed to March, 1966, was 1,470,000. If the new enthusiasm that has been generated through the program is maintained, the rate of population growth is expected to be reduced considerably by the end of the next decade.

With the population growth checked, agricultural production improved, and the vast resources harnessed for development of industry, it may be hoped that India would be solving her basic and staggering problems within the next decade or two. On the other hand, a thorough analysis of the Indian economy, which has not been possible in this context, would show that that is a rather over-simplified statement which seems to ignore the multitudes of difficulties, drawbacks and problems, each of which is an obstacle to India's journey towards a self-sustaining economy. However,

TABLE 3

PATTERNS OF PROGRESS IN PLANNING: EDUCATION AND HEALTH

	Unit	1950-51	1955-56 (End of 1st Plan)	% Inc.	1960-61 (End of 2nd Plan)	% Inc.	1965-66 (End of 3rd Plan)	% Inc.	1970-71 (End of 4th Plan)	% Inc.
EDUCATION										
General education in schools	Millions	23.5	31.3	32.99	44.7	42.93	67.7	51.62	97.5	44.0
Technical Education										
a. Engineering i) Degree	Thousands	4.1	5.9	43.80	13.8	133.89	24.7	78.93	30.0	20.0
ii) Diploma	Thousands	5.9	10.5	77.96	25.8	46.67	49.9	93.41	68.0	36.0
b. Agricultural: degree level	Numbers	1,060	1,989	87.64	5,634	183.28	8,936	53.59	11,500	
c. Veterinary: degree level	Numbers	434	1,269	192.39	1,300	2.44	1,319	1.46		
HEALTH										
Hospitals and dispensaries	Thousands	8.6	10.0	16.28	12.6	28.00	14.6	16.67		
Hospital beds	Thousands	113	125	10.62	186	48.80	240	29.03	300	25.0
Primary health units	Numbers		725		2,800	286.91	4,800	71.43	5,200	8.3
Family planning centers	Numbers		147		1,649	1217.68	11,474	595.81	48,405	321.9
Nurses registered	Thousands	15.0	18.5	23.33	27.0	45.84	45.0	68.67	87.0	93.3
Doctors practicing	Thousands	56.0	65.9	17.68	70.0	6.22	86.0	22.56	131.0	52.3

TABLE 4

PATTERNS OF PROGRESS IN PLANNING: NATIONAL INCOME AND POPULATION

	Unit	1950-51	1955-56 (End of 1st Plan)	% Inc.	1960-61 (End of 2nd Plan)	% Inc.	1965-66 (End of 3rd Plan)	% Inc.	1970-71 (End of 4th Plan)	% Inc.
NATIONAL INCOME—POPULATION										
National Income 1960-61 Prices	Rs. millions	98,500	116,700	18.47	141,400	21.17	159,300	12.68	231,000	46.01
Per Capita Income 1960-61 Prices	Rs	275	299	8.73	326	9.03	325	-0.31	417	23.31
Population	Millions	363	398	9.64	439	10.05	498	12.53	555	12.18

SOURCE: *Weekly India News*, September 23, 1966. Information Service of India, Embassy of India, Washington, D. C.
Rs. = Rupees.

that is beside the point. India has chosen the democratic path for this journey, and as has been indicated through the general elections the people of India are willing to travel it. Various facets of this democratic experiment, ranging from the Five-Year plans to the Community Development projects have given them opportunities to take part in this great developmental process. They have shared the enthusiasm and responsibility of planning, the ardor and sacrifice to carry out these plans, the bitterness and disappointments of failure, and the exultation and satisfaction of success. They are conscious of the intensity and gravity of the problems, but at the same time are also aware of the attempts that are being made to overcome them. Considered from this point of view, the economic achievements of India as narrated in this chapter assume a special significance. Undoubtedly the material achievements of the three plan periods have strengthened their faith in democratic way of life and their determination to cooperate with and take part in this process. But apart from that, the efforts that have been acknowledged by the people of India, and the fact that they have been a part of these efforts, have made them even more proud, conscious, and confident of themselves and of democracy.

CHAPTER VII

Red China's Attack on India—
A Blessing in Disguise

In order to probe the causes and motives of Red Chinese aggression against India in October, 1962, it is necessary to allude briefly to some historical events relating to India, Red China and Tibet, which latter until recently was an autonomous, though not a sovereign state. This analysis will show that Red China's illegitimate claim to a few thousand square miles of mountain territory covered with snow and ice was motivated by her imperialistic design and her unsuccessful attempt to thrust a Communistic ideology on Indian democracy. Mao Tse-Tung, who claims to be the unrivalled leader of International Communism and Chinese-brand Marxism, and who firmly believes in violence as the only means of subjugating the free world, for years had been instigating the Indian Communist Party to infiltrate Indian politics and to capture power.

There are no two opinions possible about the fact that Red China, recognized as a potential threat to world peace, has imperialistic designs. Dictator Mao has openly declared these intentions. Although Red China began her violent excursions much earlier, during the Korean crisis in fact, India did not become aware of the danger of Communistic imperialism for a long time. True to the ideals of universal brotherhood, love and peace, India has not only cherished world peace, but has attempted to bring it about through the United Nations Organization by the adoption of policies of mediation, negotiation and reconciliation. India's policy of nonalignment has always been honest and free of selfish motives. But India's honesty and her desire for peace have not only been misunderstood by Red China, but have always been exploited by

her ever since India recognized the Chinese Communist government. Whereas India throughout has been honest in her dealings
with Red China, the latter throughout has been dishonest, de-
signing and deceitful. The complacency of India was shaken only
with the attack of the Red Chinese forces in October, 1962, and
the subsequent disillusionment of India therefore was a blessing
in disguise. In what other ways this aggression was a hidden blessing will become evident.

Before I explore the salutary effects of the Red attack, I would
like to clarify the issue of the so-called Indo-Chinese frontier dispute. Much misunderstanding has been created by the propaganda
machinery of Red China on this issue. Even in the U.S. Red
Chinese friends and agents propagated the idea that India's stand
was unjustified. These persons were most perturbed when America
acted as a true friend of India and of democracy and rushed to
help India when the situation became grave. American statesmanship and insight with regard to this crisis must be admired. In
spite of subversive propaganda put out by the Red Chinese, and
in spite of many other hurdles, America acted wisely in supporting
India both morally and materially at the critical juncture. But this
friendly act was justified also because the so-called "border dispute"
was only a blind under which Red China's imperialistic designs
were concealed. This fact will become clearer if we glance at the
historical background of the situation.

First, as a matter of fact, the frontier Red China has been claiming is not on the border of Red China territory but on the border
of Tibet, which until 1959 was an independent country. The inhabitants of Tibet are culturally, lingually and racially different
from the Chinese and have greater affinity and cultural ties with
India than with China. Unfortunately in 1950 when it appealed
to the United Nations Organization for the protection of its autonomy from Red Chinese threats, no nation but India was prepared
to support this small but strategically most important country,
which could have been granted sovereign status and protection
from Red Chinese aggression. When India realized that her lonely
support of Tibet in the United Nations would be a cry in the
wilderness, she was compelled to withdraw her sponsorship. The
result was that at this critical moment Tibet's request to the United
Nations to devise ways and means to safeguard her national interests from being jeopardized by Red Chinese aggression was shelved

indefinitely. Tibet was therefore forced by the travesty of circumstances to mortgage her freedom and to enter into a humiliating seventeen-point treaty with Red China to avoid wholesale destruction. In spite of the fact that from the ancient past Tibet had remained independent and had never been subjugated by Chinese rule, she had to accept the sovereignty of Red China under duress. It was in November of 1950 that Tibet submitted her appeal to the United Nations, pointing out that the Red Chinese were forcing Tibet to be included within the folds of Communism at the point of the sword, and that the invasion of Tibet by Communist China would be an act of grossest aggression. In March, 1951, under the pressure of the military threat of Red China, whose armed troops had already been stationed near Lhasa, the capital of Tibet, the Dalai Lama, the Tibetan head of state, had to sign the humiliating agreement which virtually meant the merging of Tibet with Red China, though Tibet's regional autonomy was accepted by Peking in that agreement. This agreement stipulated that the Chinese central government would give complete freedom to Tibet with regard to her political institutions and internal administration, but its foreign affairs were to be controlled by the Chinese central government and the Chinese army was to stay in Tibet under the pretext of "strengthening national defense." The Chinese central government recognized the position of the Dalai Lama and would maintain it according to the same agreement. The Tibetan regional government was expected to carry out reforms in administration without any directive from the Chinese central government. According to another clause in this agreement a Chinese military and administrative commission as well as a military headquarters were to be set up in Tibet to see that the terms of the agreement were carried out.

This agreement reduced Tibet to a mere "regional autonomous state" within the framework of the Chinese central Communist government. Even the regional autonomy was a farce, and in due course of time all the promises of non-interference in the internal administration of Tibet were violated. Within less than two years the Red Chinese government divided Tibet into three administrative regions and established a separate military command to control the whole of the country. Gradually new roads linking Tibet with China were built and airports constructed. The whole program was called the "liberation" of Tibet by the Red Chinese. When land reforms were forcibly introduced and the religious life of the Tibetans was shattered, revolts broke out in Tibet in 1956 and 1957. The biggest one broke out in 1959 and it was mercilessly suppressed by the Red Chinese army. There followed the escape of the Dalai Lama with his relatives, his cabinet members, and some devoted followers to India where he sought refuge and where he is still living.

The rape of Tibet by Red China and the consequent sympathy of India toward the homeless Dalai Lama were no doubt the immediate cause of the hostility of Red China towards India. But even earlier, Red China had designs upon India although outwardly she professed peace, non-violence, and co-existence. Mao had a two-fold program of converting India to Communism. First, he instigated the Communist Party of India to capture political power by singing the glories of the success of Communism in Red China. Second, he wanted to use military force to achieve this objective with the expectation that an attack on India, when combined with internal sabotage by the Communist elements in the country, would successfully bring about the "liberation" of India. But, as we shall see, this twofold plan of Red China was foiled. Although this failure of Red China cost thousands of lives, panic, suffering and even humiliation, it has proved beneficial in many ways.

Before I dilate upon the beneficial consequences of this aggression, I would also like to discuss other motives of this sudden and devastating Red attack on India. Why did Red China conclude peaceful negotiations with Burma and even with Pakistan with regard to the demarcation and the control of the border areas? Why was it that only in the case of India, which had been championing the cause of the inclusion of Red China in the United Nations Organization, should Red China resort to armed conflict for deciding the border issue? Does this mean that India is the only Asian country which believes in settling issues by violence? Does it mean that India has imperialistic designs in Tibet? These are questions which must be answered to solve the riddle of Red Chinese aggression in India. Is it not a fact that Communist tactics of gaining gradual victory over the free world are summed up in the Marxist-Leninist line, "one step backward and two steps forward"? Is it not a fact that in spite of internal dissensions between the Chinese and Russian brands of Communism historical events in the contemporary world prove that Communist blood is thicker than the water of co-existence, and that the aim of Red China has been to grab power and prestige in Asia? Answers to these questions become obvious through a dispassionate study of the progress of democracy in India and recognition of the effort of India to remain non-aligned and yet to advance economically.

I have already stated that Indian democracy—in spite of economic, social and political handicaps—has made headway and has achieved an unprecedented success in one of the most unique democratic experiments ever witnessed in human history. The problems which Red China sought to solve by the use of force, suppression and brain-washing have been tackled successfully in India gradually, peacefully and non-violently, without jeopardizing individual freedom and the democratic development of the government. Land reform in China took a heavy toll of life, although the exact statistics of murdered landowners and resisters may forever remain a mystery. In India, as I have already mentioned, the voluntary donation of land and legal acquisition through idemnification of owners of land at reasonable prices have helped the distribution of the land among the landless tillers. Whereas the heavy toll of life taken by starvation and shortages of food in Red China is not precisely known to anyone outside the Chinese iron curtain, India tided over its food shortage and managed to provide an adequate supply of food for its growing population. It is noteworthy that in 1944, when the British ruled India, a terrible famine caused the death of hundreds of thousands of men, women and children in the eastern part of the country. This famine could have been averted if the British civil servants were vigilant. But ever since the establishment of democratic government in India, no such famine has brought havoc to the country. The introduction of the latest methods of agriculture, improved seeds, mechanized farming and huge irrigation projects have changed the face of India and the fate of the farmer and the laborer. All this has happened gradually and progress is still going on. India was about to achieve self-sufficiency in food when Red China attacked her suddenly. The purpose of China's attack was unquestionably to smash the economy and the development of Indian democracy.

The other motive was to isolate India in Asia to compel her to give up her non-alignment policy and to allow Red China to become the unrivalled leader of Asia. Red China, jealous of the steady progress of Indian democracy, at the same time became apprehensive that the other uncommitted nations of Asia would take India as an ideal and convey the impression that Communism was not a superior political ideology as compared with democracy. Having once proved India an inferior country politically and morally by forcing her to join the western power bloc (and thus cut loose from the group of small non-aligned nations), Red China could "liberate" those nations and grab them very easily. This imperialistic design therefore was a motive force behind the Red Chinese attack on India. How far these motives have actually been fulfilled or satisfied has yet to be seen. But this motive certainly explains why Red China purposely resolved "her" Tibetan border disputes with Burma and Pakistan without a shot, and why she took up arms against India only. There is little doubt that Red China had been preparing for the major assault from 1950, meanwhile pretending to be India's best friend. If Red China had not entered into the Pancha Shila agreement, the agreement of peaceful co-existence with India, with a view to make India complacent towards the imperialistic designs of Mao Tse-Tung, the attack could not have been sudden, devastating, and dramatic. Moreover any indication of the aggressive nature of Communist China would have been inconsistent with the double talk and double behavior of Communist politicians. The inconsistencies of Red Chinese diplomacy and her behavior towards India are thoroughly consistent with the ethics and ideology of Communism in general and Chinese Communism in particular.

The first inconsistency which made India uneasy, but which was in fact a tipoff to the future aggressive designs of Red China, occurred within four days after India recognized the Chinese Communist government. The Indian government recognized the Red regime of China on the 29th of December, 1949, expecting that this act of goodwill would lead to international understanding not only in Asia but even in the west. The recognition of Red China by Britain certainly supported India's optimism. But it was actually to prove to be not the case. Mao Tse-Tung had many surprises in store for the promoters of peace. The Red government in Peking declared on January 1st, 1950, that the "liberation" of Tibet was the aim of the Red Chinese Army, designated "The People's Liberation Army." It was hard to grasp from whom the Red Chinese were going to "liberate" Tibet. Since the 7th century A.D.

Tibet had been a free country under an independent government, though it had been under the nominal suzerainty of China from time to time. Any study of the long checkered history of this suzerainty would reveal that Tibet was throughout independent and that at the most China had claimed to be suzerain and not a sovereign power over Tibet. Tibet had signed a treaty with Britain independently, and on a number of occasions China exchanged diplomatic missions with Tibet. In 1913 the Dalai Lama had a treaty with the sovereign state of Outer Mongolia and asserted the complete independence of Tibet in 1913. However, the British government always regarded Tibet as an autonomous country under the suzerainty of China. During World War II Tibet remained neutral and did not send her forces to China. Since 1930 a political agent of British India was stationed in Lhasa, the capital of Tibet. During the British reign over India there were Indian trade agencies in Tibet, postal-telegraph services between India and Tibet were run by the Indian government, and a small military escort was also stationed in Tibet for the protection of the commercial road. China had not even utilized her nominal suzerainty over Tibet. Hence when Red China declared that she was intent upon "liberating" Tibet, Prime Minister Nehru was quite surprised because he had expected that the suzerainty, not the sovereignty of Red China over Tibet could be settled through mediation and negotiation. This surprise changed into anxiety when in October of 1950 Red China ordered her troops to invade Tibet to "liberate" the Tibetan people from the influence of imperialists, to unify China and to protect Chinese frontiers. Exchanges of notes between the Indian government and the Red Chinese regime followed. In these notes India expressed her "surprise and regret" over the Red Chinese resorting to aggression instead of negotiation at the time when the Indian Prime Minister was trying to prevent the Korean conflict from spreading over other parts of the world. At the same time he was also making efforts to get Red China admitted to the U.N. thereby helping to promote peace in the world. The Red Chinese government, however, disagreed with the Indian viewpoint and alleged that India had been "affected by foreign influences hostile to China in Tibet."

When India pointed out that China could peacefully settle the matter with Tibetans by recognizing their autonomy and by getting the Chinese suzerainty recognized by Tibet, the Red Chinese asserted that China had sovereign rights over Tibet, and that India was unjust in standing in the way of the exercise of Chinese sovereign power over Tibet. As already mentioned, in spite of Tibet's appeal to the United Nations India could not help her, and Tibet had to accept the dictatorial terms of Red China, which did accept the autonomy of Tibet. The Dalai Lama, the refugee head of the Tibetan state, declared after his escape from Tibet that the agreement between Tibet and Red China had been signed under duress. This fact, although apprehended earlier by some Indians, was known to her leaders only in 1959.

After the agreement between Tibet and Red China had been signed in March, 1951, Red Chinese diplomats put on the masks of peace and glibly talked about co-existence. Several cultural and goodwill missions were exchanged between India and China, and much propaganda about the miraculous march of Red China towards prosperity and abundance was let loose in India by the fifth columnists of Red China. India's idealism and love for peace not only made her complacent towards Red China but prompted her to seek her goodwill. The Chinese prime minister visited India and was accorded a roaring reception. India and China signed a treaty of co-existence, later known as the "Pancha Shila Agreement," or the agreement on the "five principles of good conduct" between nations.

According to the five clauses of the Pancha Shila agreement, which was later accepted by thirty other nations of the world, the parties signing it were required (1) to recognize each other's sovereignty and territorial jurisdiction; (2) not to resort to aggression; (3) not to interfere in each other's internal affairs; (4) to maintain equality in mutual economic gain; and (5) to promote peaceful co-existence. I have elaborated the significance of these principles of national conduct in another book.* Here I would like to allude to this significance briefly. The first principle of national conduct, the recognition of the sovereignty of each nation, is based on the acceptance of truth, which is of course opposed to blatant lies, hypocrisy and propaganda. To recognize the sovereignty of an independent nation is to accept the truth of human freedom, and to honor the territorial jurisdiction of another sovereign state is to express faith and conviction in the recognition of the truth of

---

*Ethical Philosophies of India, pp. 348-50.

individual and national freedom. The second principle, i.e., the principle of non-aggression, is based on the concept of non-violence, which is not only repugnant to but diametrically opposed to violent revolution, the core of communism and the only recognized method of totalitarian victory. The third principle, non-interference in the internal policy of another country, is based on the principle of justice, which has no meaning in Communistic philosophy, since according to it suppression of individual freedom and the reduction of the individual to a mere cog in the social machinery are themselves the accepted means of keeping power. The fourth principle of equality in economic gains is based on non-stealing or respect for other's property. According to Communism not only is respect for other's property unjust, but even the possession of property is criminal. The fifth principle, peaceful co-existence, implies allowing every independent nation to practice its own political ideology and not to impose one's own ideology, Communistic or otherwise, on the other country. This basic principle would undermine the expansionistic designs of Communism in general and Red China's mission of "liberating" all the countries of the world from imperialism and capitalism in particular. India signed the agreement of Pancha Shila earnestly and honestly to promote goodwill and international understanding, and Red China did so manifestly with a view to sabotaging India and intensifying its subversive activities against the Indian nation without any fear of being doubted by the duped Indians. Moreover, this agreement was signed by Red China to get ratification for her rape of Tibet. India was trapped very cleverly. India had forgotten Gandhi's view about the Chinese nation, when more than a decade earlier than the agreement of Pancha Shila he had characterized the Chinese as unreliable and unprincipled.

The Pancha Shila agreement was the second consistent inconsistency on the part of the Red Chinese. But it hit home and worked like a charm, having a narcotic effect on the Indian nation. It led to the exchange of a series of goodwill, cultural and economic missions between India and China, and created a false impression of the wonderful success of Communism in Red China, particularly among the paper-reading masses of one state in India where literacy is highest. This was Kerala, the southernmost Indian state. The Communist party of Kerala succeeded in defeating the Congress Party in the general elections in 1957, chiefly owing to the halo of

Communist "success" in Red China created and nurtured by the exchange of the goodwill and cultural missions—all of which influenced over sixty per cent of educated masses of Kerala. It is worthy of note here that the overall percentage of literacy in India is between 15 and 20. In India every state has its own ministerial cabinet to carry on the internal administration, and this cabinet is formed by the leader of the majority party of the legislative assembly. In 1957, when the results of the general elections in Kerala were known, it was discovered that there was no absolute majority party elected in its legislature. The Communist leader, Nambudaripad, successfully won over a few independent elected legislators and gained an absolute majority for the Communist party, the largest single party returned in the general elections. He was therefore invited by the governor of Kerala to form the first democratic Communist government not only in India but in the world. Blessed by Mao and hailed by all the Communists of the world, Nambudaripad, the chief minister of Kerala, took the oath of allegiance to the Indian constitution along with his Red cabinet in the presence of the Congress-appointed governor of Kerala, flinging a surprise even to the incorrigible Marxists by converting Communism into a democracy. This was perhaps a unique example of the consistent inconsistency of Communist philosophy. However, under the garb of democracy Nambudaripad was actually planning to Communize democracy, to prepare the ground for the revolution, and to sabotage the central government of India. When public funds began to be diverted to Communistic propaganda and government machinery was used to convert the masses to the Communistic ideology, the tide turned against the now exposed Communist party in Kerala and the masses demanded the dismissal of the Red ministry. The subsequent use of force by this Red government aroused the sentiments of the people and the whole of this small state was thrown into chaos due to the highhandedness of the ministry. The result was that within a few months after the Communist party in Kerala assumed the reins of the government a state of emergency had to be declared by the president of India, and law and order had to be maintained by the national government until the next emergency elections and the dismissal of the ministry and assembly of Kerala. The consistent inconsistency of the Communist leaders was thus exposed. In the new emergency elections held in Kerala the Communist party was defeated, and the Congress Party, with the help of other parties, was successful in establishing a stable ministry in the state. This was a great blow to Communism not only in India, but also and moreso to Red China.

However, the Red Chinese government continued to pour Communist propaganda into India. She now devised a plan to send her nationals, particularly her diplomats, from her embassy in India to various functions of the Indo-China Friendship Association to contact college students and address them, even though these speakers always required English interpreters to impress upon the masses of India that Indians and Chinese were "brothers." I remember one such occasion in a college I taught at in those days. This was as recently as 1958. Two Red Chinese veterans, both most likely from the Chinese embassy in India, came to address a student gathering. One student leader who had been fascinated by the pseudo-sincerity of the Red Chinese to bring India and China together was enthusiastic about the Red guests. When one of the two veterans had spoken and the other interpreted his speech in grammatically incorrect English, the speaker asked the audience to join him in a slogan of goodwill which he uttered in the Hindi language. Now it is almost impossible for Chinese to learn Hindi, which is now the national language of India, as it is almost impossible for the Indians to learn the Chinese language. The slogan was "Hindi Chini bhai bhai" i.e. "Indians and Chinese are brothers." These Chinese veterans could not pronounce the word "bhai" correctly. Instead of saying "bhai" (which means brother), they said "bye." Hence they shouted to the audience, "Hindi Chini bye bye," which meant in Hindi that Indians and Chinese should bid good-bye to each other!

Double-talk and double-dealing are the keynotes of Red China's policy. When the mask of democracy failed to convert India to Communism, and when in the general elections of 1962 Red China found that the Indian masses voted for democracy, the only way open to her was to employ violence and aggression, so she invaded India. Even here adherence to blatant lies and consistent inconsistency was prominent. While the Red Chinese heavily equipped forces were attacking India and creating havoc in Indian territory, the Peking radio kept announcing that Indians were attacking Chinese. Even when the Red Chinese had entered the Assam valley, the Peking radio alleged that India was the aggressor. The most obvious contradiction was that the same radio station announced soon after that the Red Chinese forces were withdrawing in spite of having conquered Indian territory. Thousands of Indian soldiers were killed for they were unprepared and were heavily outnumbered. The Red Chinese had the advantage of using the latest mechanized weapons (which could not be manufactured by Red China); they had also the advantage of occupying higher ground. There were however, numerous examples of the bravery of Indian soldiers who sacrificed their lives in the defense of their motherland. Their undaunted courage and patriotism kept up the morale of the Indian people.

The purpose of Red China's attack, as I have said, was ultimately to show that Communism could make a nation stronger and more prosperous in a shorter time than democracy. The Chinese Communists expected that their counterparts in India would help them in creating internal disturbances, most likely in Bengal, which was very near the scene of fighting. But the sudden arousal of the feeling of patriotism in the whole of India, the voluntary donation of wealth and the voluntary enlistment of hundreds of thousands of young people to fight for the freedom of India to the death shattered the hopes of subversion and sabotage on the part of the Communists. No Communist would dare oppose the current of patriotism which suddenly awakened and united India against the danger of Communist domination. In the meantime the United States and Britain came to the timely rescue of the Indians by the immediate supply of the latest weapons which the Indian army sorely lacked. American aid and the promptness with which it was rushed to the stormed border were the factors which made the aggressor change his mind and declare a unilateral cease-fire immediately. The unilateral declaration, the resolution to withdraw from a part of the occupied area, and the effrontery to dictate the terms of treaty after the disastrous attack and repulse were events which suprised everyone. But I have already stated that such inconsistencies are most consistent with Red Chinese strategy and tactics. They offered to withdraw from Indian territory and gave their own definition of the Indian border, which excluded more territory than they had unjustly claimed. They declared a unilateral cease fire, but refused to come to any agreement through negotiation. The danger of a more fierce attack at any moment still looms large over India, and suspense and tension still prevail without any hope of peaceful settlement of the issue. Whereas Red China has rejected all the proposals of peaceful settlement of the Indian border made either by India or by other neutral nations, she immediately concluded a treaty with Pakistan on the border issue. This dramatic move is again consistent with the inconsistencies of Red China. If Red China could stab the back of India, a non-aligned country which has been championing her inclusion in the United Nations, how loyal and true she will be to Pakistan and how far she will honor the clauses of that treaty are moot questions.

What blessing if any can be attributed to the near catastrophe of the Red attack on India? I can see four good results: (1) the new unity of India; (2) the death of Communism in India; (3) the disillusionment of India with regard to the pretensions of co-existence on the part of some countries, and (4) an inexhaustible fund of goodwill for the United States on the part of the masses of India. Let me say a few words about these effects of the Indo-Chinese undeclared war.

The immediate and strongest effect of the sudden attack on the Indian people was the revival of a spirit of unity and a strong urge to hazard all for the maintenance of hard-earned freedom. This spirit had previously been exhibited during India's non-violent struggle for independence, during which thousands of Indians sacrificed their lives, and millions underwent the ordeals of jail and the loss of property. Millions of rupees were donated voluntarily to the Indian National Congress, which was the only political organization fighting for the freedom of the country. This spirit of self-devotion and self-sacrifice had been dormant in the Indians for a decade largely on account of differences on the issue of language and demarcation of the boundaries of states. But the danger of the Red dragon immediately aroused the dormant spirit of unity among Indians young and old, and all the differences of caste, creed, religion, language and state were forgotten. Indians young or old, rich or poor, male or female, voluntarily donated money, gold and ornaments for the defense of India. Government employees offered voluntary deductions from their salaries, and whole families offered voluntary enlistment in the army. Enormous amounts of gold and precious stones were donated by women who took a vow to go without jewelry for the defense of the nation. Retired military personnel enthusiastically rejoined the Indian army, and every individual was ready to sacrifice his life if he were required to do so. This firm determination of the Indians and their strong urge to give their treasure and shed their last drop of blood for national defense demoralized the Red Chinese and the fifth columnists of Red China.

It was most natural for the masses of India to express their resentment against the Communist party of India which had all the while been supporting the Red Chinese view of the border issue. It became obvious that Indian Communists were imposters and were in league with the Red Chinese. It was anticipated that in the event of the entry of Red Chinese into the plains of India they would sabotage and take up arms against their own countrymen. In spite of the declaration of some Indian Communists that the Red Chinese attack was an aggression, the masses of India did not trust them and would not tolerate the sight of the Communists. The Communists were stoned when they made public appearances, and a natural hatred for the Communist party in India and its sympathisers was one obvious outcome of the Red attack. The resignation of Mr. Krishna Menon was the demand of the masses, and it had to be conceded. This awakening among the millions of Indian citizens who realized that Communism in its naked form means injustice, aggression and imperialism of the worst sort, has brought about the political death of the Communist party of India and of its sympathisers. Thus the Red Chinese attack proved suicidal for Communism in India. India is united today, and this unity is directed against Communist aggression from outside and Communist sabotage from inside.

There is a Hindi verse which says that courage, virtue, friend and wife are to be tested only in a crisis. If all four stand by us in time of calamity, they are true and reliable. If they fail to help us then, they are untrue and unreliable. India's darkest hour was therefore the hour of test not only for her but also for those who posed as her friends, admirers of her moral stand and her ideal of coexistence. The United States and the United Kingdom were truly perturbed at the misfortune of India. They rushed arms to India in time and gave her courage and strength. India came to know her friends. This brought about a sudden arousal of the feelings of love and goodwill among the masses of India for the United States and the United Kingdom. Since India is a member of the Commonwealth and Britain was expected to assist her, the goodwill for the United States among the Indians today is deeper and stronger than ever before in the history of India. This inexhaustible fund of goodwill and fond regard for the people of United States on the part of the average man of India has brought these two nations very close to each other. Communist propaganda attempts to dub the United States an "imperialist" nation cannot wipe out the favorable image of America from the mind of the average man of India. India, which is a democracy on trial and is prepared to stand all the tests to preserve freedom, equality and justice, is undoubtedly one of the greatest bulwarks against the march of totalitarians in the free world. Not only the United States, but all the other democracies big and small must understand the intentions of India if the cause of democracy is to be defended in the world today.

This fact leads us to discuss whether the Kashmir issue is a help or hindrance in the defense of democracy in India.

CHAPTER VIII

The Kashmir Issue:
Indo-Pakistan Relations

India and Pakistan are twin nations, having been born and having attained independence from Britain on the same day. It surprises the outside world to find that these geographically proximate and culturally similar countries, which form the largest sub-continent of Asia, do not see eye to eye in political matters. In spite of the fact that both countries are members of the British Commonwealth, have a common border, and have similar economic and social problems, they seldom agree in international matters and sometimes, whether in the United Nations or in the meetings of the British Commonwealth, oppose each other bitterly. Most students of political science would concede that in the interest of democracy in Asia and even in their own mutual social, political, economic and cultural interest, these two countries should work in unison in their march to prosperity and in their opposition to the Red menace in Asia. What is the main reason for these two countries pulling in different ways and sometimes adopting foreign policies which seem diametrically opposed to each other? Pakistan asserts that the Kashmir issue is the only bone of contention between the two countries, and that once this problem is solved the relations between India and Pakistan would be cordial. Many Westerners seem to be convinced of this view, which has systematically and most vigorously been propagated by Pakistan. Although Pakistan also accuses India of imperialist designs and dramatically poses as fearful of aggression from non-aligned India, yet her constant complaint has been that Kashmir belongs to her and that she must "liberate" Kashmir from India. There are countless misunderstandings about the Kashmir stalemate among Westerners due to lack of knowledge about the whole issue, and due also to the propaganda of Pakistan against India, who on account of her inherent pacifism has never tried to retaliate to the extent of making open efforts to falsify the charges of Pakistan. Before drawing any conclusions a factual historical background of the whole matter will be presented. This will help the reader to judge for himself the merits and the demerits of the case, and will also enable him to understand the importance of co-operation between India and Pakistan not only for their own sake, but also for the sake of the general cause of peace, freedom and democracy.

I have already stated that before India became independent there were 562 princely states whose internal administration was entirely in the hands of the hereditary aristocratic rulers. Kashmir, a beautiful state in northern India touching the borders of Tibet, was one of the princely states given the option by the British government either to join India or to join Pakistan or to remain sovereign after August 15, 1947. The other princely states which were geographically within India or within Pakistan merged into India and Pakistan respectively with the consent of their rulers. Kashmir, whose borders touched both India and Pakistan had not yet decided which country it was going to join. Since the repercussions of the partition of India and Pakistan brought havoc, and since the fanaticism of the Muslim League in Pakistan had resulted in the massacre and extermination of Hindus and Sikhs from West Pakistan—resulting in a retalitation in the East Punjab area of India—the Hindu ruler of Kashmir watched and waited. He maintained law and order in his state and there is no evidence that even a single Muslim migrated from that state to Pakistan out of fear of Hindu reprisals. Not only the Muslims in Kashmir, but millions of Muslims in other princely states and provinces of India decided to live in India. The Muslim League was not representative of all Indian Muslims. It was an instrument for creating rifts, fanning bigotry and fanaticism, and raising the slogan, "Islam in danger", to hamper nationalism in India. The Indian National Congress, the true representative political organization, agreed to partition as a last resort to weed out the few fanatic leaders like Mr. Jinnah, and to see India flourish as a secular state, without any distinction of caste, creed, and religion. That is why *fifty million* Muslims did *not* opt for Pakistan. They continue to be nationals of India to this day. In the face of these facts the ruler of Kashmir was justified in being cautious of the fury of fanaticism which would have brought havoc to the people of his state. Moreover by not deciding immediately which country his state would join, he was exercising the legal right granted him by the British government.

But the Muslim League government of Pakistan determined to take Kashmir by force. In 1947 Pakistan suddenly attacked Kashmir. The Pakistan forces, along with hordes of hired frontier tribes of Pakistan, advanced into the valley of Kashmir killing, looting, and destroying town after town and village after village, setting everything on fire. The aggressors reached the precincts of Srinagar, the capital of Kashmir, and had devastated about three-fourths of the state territory. The ruler of Kashmir flew to New Delhi and formally requested the Indian government to accept the merger of Kashmir with India and to save Kashmir from the aggressors. The Indian government acted promptly and dispatched Indian troops to Kashmir. Within three days the aggressors were turned out of two-thirds of Kashmir. It would probably have taken Indian soldiers a few more days to expel the aggressors from the whole territory of Kashmir, for after the legel merger of Kashmir with India there was no question of any external country (like Pakistan) interfering in the internal affairs of India. But our honest and perhaps over-scrupulous prime minister, Nehru, brought the complaint to the United Nations Organization, pointing out the naked aggression of Pakistan in Kashmir. Had India not brought the matter to the United Nations there would have been no international problem at all. Having once referred the Kashmir issue to U.N. it became necessary to await its verdict and agree to a cease-fire.

With the passage of time the Kashmir issue became a stalemate. In the meantime India made headway as a secular democracy. She conducted three general elections successfully over the country. Moreover the elected constituent Assembly of Kashmir as well ratified the merger of Kashmir and India, although such a ratification was unnecessary in view of the legal merger of Kashmir by the ruler in 1947—which was the pattern for all the other mergers of the princely states. It is very important to clarify the word "secular" as the adjective used to describe the Indian state. Without clarification of this term much misunderstanding is bound to arise with regard to India's stand on Kashmir. Western countries tend to forget the importance of India as a "secular state" from the first day of her independence. In view of the presence of almost all the religions of mankind in India it was essential to keep the state and politics uncontaminated by a religious bias. The Indian National Congress was committed to the secular nature of the Indian state even before the attainment of independence. During the past nineteen years India has successfully made progress as a secular state granting full religious freedom to all her citizens and having had no interference in political and governmental matters from any religion whatsoever.

The net result of adherence to the secular ideal is that all the citizens of India have an equal opportunity to develop politically, socially and economically. Not only Muslims, but Christians, Parsis, Sikhs, Jainas and Buddhists benefit equally by the secular democracy of India. Thousands of Muslims are active politicians. Hundreds of them are the members of state legislative assemblies and the central parliament. Muslims in India are also ministers of state cabinets and the central cabinets. They are high court judges, governors, ambassadors and diplomats. They occupy other high posts in government and administration. They are businessmen, industrialists, engineers, doctors and prominent educators. The Vice-president of India today is a well-know Muslim, Dr. Zaqir Hussain, who was previously the Vice-chancellor of the Muslim university and also a state governor. Whereas in Pakistan not a single Hindu occupies any administrative position in a state legislature or cabinet, the Muslims in India are most highly placed in all spheres. Whereas suppression of non-Muslims continues to be the policy of the theocratic state of Pakistan (which did not hold a single general election for over sixteen years) Indian democracy has proved to be most successful as a secular government. This success of democracy and the emergence of India as one nation devoted to the well-being and freedom of all citizens without distinction of caste, creed and religion cannot be and should not be brushed aside as an accident in the political history of India. It has cost India much effort, exertion and self-sacrifice, especially in the face of the naked injustice, disparity and fanaticism prevailing in Pakistan, which preaches hatred for India and makes ceaseless efforts to encourage fanaticism in order to jeopardize Indian democracy. Neither India nor any other sane nation in the world would foster fanaticism to bring about disunity, disorder and hatred among its people by raising the slogan "religion in danger" in the present age. Fifty million Muslims in India (a number which is more than fifty percent of the population of Pakistan) continue to be Indian citizens, enjoying not only equal privileges but sometimes special privileges. The fanaticism and madness which were the cause of fratricide in 1947 are relics of the ugly history of India, and any attempt to revive them would be a heinous crime.

The Kashmir issue should be studied dispassionately with reference to the facts mentioned above. As I have stated, millions of Muslims, Christians, Sikhs, Parsis, Jainas and Buddhists live in India. All are well-represented in the Indian parliament and government. There are intermarriages between various communities and in due course of time India expects to achieve ethnic integration. This integration is bound to be jeopardized if any attempt is made to hand over any part of Kashmir to Pakistan simply because there are fifty-five Muslims for every forty-five Hindus and Sikhs living there. If we were to repartition India on a purely religious basis only, as Pakistanis argue we should in Kashmir, what would happen to the fifty million Muslims living in all other states of India? What if fanaticism and communal madness were to spread as a result of the revival of religious dissensions? Moreover, why shouldn't other religious communities demand separate states? In that case, would it be desirable to divide India into a hundred or so pieces? There would be no end to the demand of new states on the basis of religious communal and denominational differences. The reader should study the whole issue dispassionately from this perspective.

As a matter of fact in their heart of hearts the Pakistani diplomats realize that no democracy can flourish based on religion or fanaticism. It is strange that the Muslim League, the sole creator of the theocratic state of Pakistan, has disappeared in the present administration of Pakistan herself. Is this not an indication that religious bias has been considered dangerous for government and for the economic advancement of a new nation even by Pakistan? Then why does Pakistan claim Kashmir only on religious grounds? Having abolished the League, the creator of religious, Islamic Pakistan, the leaders of that country are harping on the "liberation" of the Muslims of Kashmir, thereby following a Nazi tactic of expanding their territory. It is a strange contradiction—stranger than Communism's consistent inconsistency. India does not want Pakistan fragmented. On the contrary, Indian democracy can be secure and strong when there are stronger democracies on her border. Indian leaders realized this fact even in 1947. It is one reason why India gave five hundred and fifty million rupees to Pakistan to start with, although this act of prompt generosity resulted in the assassination of the father of Indian nation, Mahatma Gandhi, because of a misinterpretation of this policy on the part of one fanatic. These facts, which are consistent with India's policy of non-violence, love and non-aggression, should not be lost sight of. The Messianic attitude of Pakistan to "liberate" Muslims can have no end, even if Kashmir or a part of it were to be unjustifiably handed over to her.

What then is the possible solution to the hostilities between India and Pakistan? How can these geographically close, culturally akin and politically inter-related twin nations of the Indian sub-continent be reconciled? How can they avoid the menace of Red China which might take advantage of the rift between them? A realistic attitude is undoubtedly essential on the part of both countries. Such an attitude demands that the interest of democracy and of the economic well-being of the people of both the countries be given priority. India has never made any attempt to harm Pakistan or to coerce her in any manner, whereas Pakistan accuses India of imperialistic designs and falsely propagates the notion in the West that she was expecting an attack from India any moment. India has not complained of Pakistan's military development. If India had any desire to attack Pakistan, she would not have brought the Kashmir issue to the United Nations. On the contrary, she could easily have entered Pakistan with her superior and larger military force and would have converted the Kashmir issue into a civil war. It would have been a matter of a few days to conquer Pakistan and to reunite it with India even with the support of the disgruntled refugees on both sides and with the aid of the nationalist Frontier province in 1947. But that never was nor is it the aim of the Indian nation. As I have already stated, it is the earnest desire of Indians to see Pakistan flourish as a true democracy. The Indian people, including Indian Muslims as well, never wished ill even to the British during the struggle for independence. How could they wish ill to Pakistan, which was physically, geographically, socially, politically, and culturally a part of India, and which was voluntarily allowed to separate with a view to get rid of ill-will and misunderstandings? Mr. Jinnah, the father of Pakistan, always falsely accused the Indian National Congress of being a Hindu body. But even after the physical partition of India, even after the Muslim League turned out all Hindus and Sikhs from West Pakistan, the Indian National Congress did not take reprisals. Had it been a merely communal body, or had it even the least idea of retaliating against the Muslim League, it could very easily have exported all the Muslims from India to Pakistan—even peacefully. Not only the Congress Party as a political party, but Indian Hindus are not communal. There are some communal parties in India. They have also been fighting elections for the past sixteen years. But none of them has been able to make any headway either in state legislatures or in the central parliament. The Hindu Mahasabha, which was the antidote to the Muslim league, is a defunct organization in India. Strangely enough, the Muslim League, which has died out in Pakistan, has a political existence in India and has not been outlawed in secular India. Had Hindus been communal-minded they would have voted a communal organization into power. These facts falsify the blatant claims of the late Mr. Jinnah and his political successors who are still following the tactics of false propaganda and cheap popularity by dubbing the secular Indian state a "Hindu state". As long as the aim of the Pakistan leaders, whether they be democrats or autocrats, remains the holding of power (at the cost of democracy), and as long as they go on repeating the hackneyed slogans of "Islam in danger" and "India a Hindu state", there can be no way of solving the deadlock. Such an attitude is not only false but most unrealistic and damaging more to Pakistan than to India, because the latter is a real democracy and secular state whereas the former is a theocracy and not yet a democracy.

The unrealistic attitude of Pakistan leaders sometimes passes all limits and clearly reveals mere hatred and jealousy which are undermining the interests of Pakistan. When Red China attacked India, Pakistan leaders were jubilant. Mr. Ayub Khan, the chief administrator of Pakistan, went to the extent of saying that the attack had been exaggerated by India and that Nehru had made a mountain out of a molehill. Not only this, Mr. Khan said that there were two potential dangers to Asia, Chinese communism and Indian imperialism. He went on to add that Indian imperialism was more dangerous than Chinese communism. This declaration was published in *New York Times* during the Red Chinese aggression. No sane man would accept such views. But it was therefore natural for Pakistan to conclude a treaty with Red China on their border issue. When the United States spontaneously sent aid to India in her distress, Pakistan protested and went to the extent of threatening betrayal of the western bloc. She objected to aircraft carrying weapons to India passing over her territory. Another piece of false and malicious propaganda designed to obstruct United States arms aid to India was the argument that India might use these weapons against Pakistan. In other words, Pakistan alleged that India would prefer to attack Pakistan and allow herself to be conquered by Red China. So far Pakistan has been blackmailing and getting all possible concessions and aid from the U.S. by exaggerating her distress and by harping on India's intention to attack her. History itself is witness to the sincerity of India. If India did not attack Pakistan at the time she could (assuming she had a mind to do so) and when she was in no danger from Red China, how on earth could she conceivably attack Pakistan, a member of SEATO and CENTO, when the red dragon loomed large over her?

Thus all these accusations and allegations are not only false and imaginary but damaging. The present situation demands a realistic and pragmatic attitude on the part of Pakistan. It is high time for Pakistan's leaders to shed the false fanatic propaganda, to stop shouting hackneyed slogans, and to offer a hand of friendship to India. India will respond with warmth and love and will do her best to repay such timely sympathy materially by aiding Pakistan. Why should she not consider herself the younger sister of India and ask India to share her joys and sorrows? I repeat, my only purpose in relating all these bitter facts is to draw a realistic picture and to help bring about real understanding between India and Pakistan.

It is worth noting that there are many other Muslim countries in Asia. Afghanistan and Persia are the oldest Muslim countries, and Burma, Malaya, Indonesia, Ceylon and Thailand are all non-Hindu countries. None of these countries has ever said that India has any aggressive design or that India's policy is harmful to them. Even Islamic countries like Iran and Afghanistan, which are virtually all Muslim, have never accused India as the enemy of Islam. They have very cordial relations with India and admire her.

Pakistan is the only country which carries on fierce propaganda against India in and out of season. Here is one specific example (*New York Times* Western edition, July 9, 1963):

"Rawalpindi, Pakistan. July 8, 1963 (Reuters)—President Mohammed Ayub Khan warned today that small Asian nations would be driven to seek the 'protection' of communist China if Western arms support to India continued. President Ayub Khan said at a political meeting that the West was contributing to the spread of Communism in Asia by forcing into Chinese arms nations that feared a strong India. He included the Soviet Union in his criticism. Moscow and the West have moved to bolster India since Communist China attacked her northern border last year. The Unted States and Britain, President Ayub Khan said, are 'overoptimistic' in hoping smaller Asian nations will look to India after her military strength has been built up."

This statement is indicative of the extreme prejudice and malice of Mr. Ayub Khan. Even a layman without any background of the political situation of the world would be surprised to read the words "protection of Communist China". It is incredible that Ayub Khan thinks Red China will protect the smaller nations of Asia, when she has imperialistic designs on India, the largest Asian democracy. Presumably he is either expressing his own feeling that Communist China is the protector of other countries and that India is the aggressor, or he is only trying to dupe Western diplomats by bringing a baseless and most ridiculous allegation against India. If the statement is a sincere statement, it is certainly something more than a mere allegation or propaganda. "Small Asian nations would be driven to seek the 'protection' of Communist China, if Western arms support to India continued," implies that the conquest of India by Red China (imminent if India is weakened by the stoppage of Western arms aid) would be joyful tidings for the small Asian nations. Does it imply that small Asian nations consider India a tyrant, and hence that Red China, the "protector" of the weak, is justified in conquering India? No other nation has ever expressed such vindictive and inconsistent ideas about India. If the leading statesman of Pakistan utters such irresponsible, illogical and baseless statements, how successfully can he guide the destinies of his people? How far can the "guided democracy" of Pakistan march forward in the nuclear age under the leadership of such a self-elected president? is a question the reader should try to answer himself. If the statement is not sincere and is merely an indirect expression of the resentment of Mr. Ayub Khan toward the friendly gestures of Britain and U.S.A. vis-à-vis India at the most critical juncture of the Red menace, then the West should beware the sincerity of Pakistan. If such is the case Pakistan might go to any length to oppose India and to see her humiliated and even conquered by Red China. Given her treaty with Red China, Pakistan might decide to back out of SEATO and CENTO, particularly if India were to sign these treaties.

However, the best interest of Pakistan herself is to give up her unrealistic attitude toward India and shed her malice. These tactics of duping the masses of Pakistan by hackneyed slogans on the part of leaders like Ayub Khan are detrimental to the interests of democracy. The need of the hour is to foster cooperation rather than estrangement among the Asian democracies.

I have stated more than once that in spite of the political differences between India and Pakistan, cultural ties and geographical unity remain intact. The cultural and even social relations of these two countries will probably never be severed. In fact, I am hopeful that some day these very relations will lead to mutual understanding and goodwill between India and Pakistan. I will illustrate here with reference to my personal experience how cultural relations transcend political differences. I have already mentioned that I was born in Pakistan and that I had very close relations with many politically important and religiously staunch Muslims. When the partition of India was announced and riots broke out in and around my native city, I was often at the houses of these Muslim friends without being disturbed by the riots. When no Hindu would dare pass through the area inhabited by Muslims, I used to visit my Muslim friends. While coming back to my house I was escorted safely by armed Muslims.

I was sincerely advised by these friends to migrate to India even before the partition of the country was effected and before the most furious rioting in the whole of the state of Punjab began. I was not only advised, but safely escorted by some of these Muslim friends (at the risk of their own lives) to the border of India. I was accompanied by all the members of my family, yet my parents insisted that they remain in the ancestral house. Like many other Hindus they hoped that after Pakistan attained independence they might be allowed to live there peacefully. Nevertheless, for our own safety they wanted me to leave with my five sisters. Although I apprehended that ultimately they should have to be evacuated, I agreed not to oppose them because all my other relations, my uncle and his family members, also did not want to leave. I arrived in India on August 4, 1947, and wholesale massacre in the Pakistan part of Punjab began on August 11, 1947. There was no way to know whether my parents were safe. After one month, however, I received information that they were, and I wrote my Muslim friends in Pakistan. They were kind enough to arrange the safe evacuation of my parents. However, it was impossible for Hindus to leave the Hindu locality and to reach either the railway station or the airport without danger, having to pass through thickly populated Muslim localities where rioting, fanatic Muslims were always present to attack them. My affectionate and brave Muslim friends conveyed my parents safely to the airport under an armed private guard. They faced difficulties in preventing the rioters from attacking my parents. There are countless other cases in which Muslims helped Hindus to be evacuated or to be conveyed to camps protected by the military when these camps were later organized. Similarly, many Hindus saved the lives of their neighbor Muslims in India at the risk of their own lives during those days of fury.

Now that these events are behind us, cultural ties are stronger and the reunion of old friends and relations, though hampered and delayed because of passport difficulties, is most exciting and thrilling. There is an important place of pilgrimage of Hindus in the city of Multan, situated in Punjab in the heart of West Pakistan. There are two very large Hindu temples there, one in the center of town and the other outside town, and both have historical and religious importance for Hindus. The temple outside the city is more important because it is built in memory of a great Hindu devotee, Bhagta Prahlad, and it is shrine for Hindus all over India. This temple is built next to a Muslim temple (Dargah) which also is a place of pilgrimage for Muslims in West Pakistan. These two temples have existed side by side for centuries, and there has never been any conflict between Hindus and the Muslims although the time of worship in both the temples has coincided, and although the ringing of the bells in the Hindu temple at the time of Muslim worship could be taken to be a cause of contention. Every year thousands of Hindus gathered in that temple on a particular day. After the partition the Pakistan government, having respect for the sentiments of Hindus, put their temple under its protection. A year after independence a huge group of Hindu pilgrims from India was allowed to hold its usual annual religious meeting there, and ever since this practice has continued. Hundreds of Hindus go there every year and stay for about a week. Similarly, thousands of Muslims from Pakistan come to an Indian city, Ajmer, to celebrate their religious festival in a Muslim monastery.

The first group of Hindus to celebrate the religious festival in Multan (West Pakistan) was a selected group, most of whom were the acknowledged leaders of Multan. When the group reached the city it was accorded a grand welcome by the local Muslim leaders. They were invited to lunch and given a civic reception. It is a recorded fact that when the Hindu group arrived in Multan and the Muslim leaders received and embraced the Hindus, they actually shed tears. The most prominent Muslim leaders said in so many words, "We feel your absence and realize that it was a great blunder on our part to allow you to leave Pakistan. Now we feel your presence would have been a great asset to the economic progress of our country." A majority of Hindus in Punjab were businessmen, bankers and industrialists. The Muslims, particularly the farmers (who formed the majority of Muslims), depended upon the mercantile talent of the Hindus. Genuine cooperation previously existed between the businessminded and industrialist Hindus and the farming Muslims, and the division of labor between these two communities was most helpful to Punjab, the most propersous state of India from the point of view of agriculture and food production. Hindus were not dominating but cooperating with Muslims to develop industry. Many Muslims had joined Hindus in setting up various industries, and gradually they were learning industry and business. In turn Hindus and Sikhs were becoming farmers. Hence the remarks of the Muslim leaders of Multan were not merely based on sentiment, but were also expression of realism. It would certainly have been beneficial for Pakistan to have allowed these non-Muslims to remain nationals of Pakistan, just as fifty million Muslims continued to remain nationals of India. But the leaders of Pakistan reversed the procedure. They harassed non-Muslims and created conditions to force them to leave their homes in Pakistan in utter disgust and frustration. Had Pakistan adopted the same democratic attitude as India she would have not only been justified in claiming Kashmir, but Kashmir would have become an integral part of Pakistan from the very beginning. The solution to all problems arising between India and Pakistan lies in a dipassionate approach, a realistic attitude and recognition of cultural kinship of both the countries.

After the successful march towards social, political and economic solidarity as a secular democracy, and after wiping out the wounds inflicted decades ago by fanaticism, communalism and the provocative sloganeering of "Islam in danger" India would at no cost and under no circumstances revive that madness by acceding to any demand of Pakistan for partitioning on a communal basis. After the establishment of a national democracy India would be ill-advised to subdivide on a religious or communal basis. Had secularism not been successful in India, had there been any communal disturbances during the political elections in any part of India, India might justifiably have been marked as a non-secular state. Had any Muslim in India been debarred from contesting elections or from making social, political and economic progress, Pakistan's stand on Kashmir on communal grounds might have been justified. But in the presence of justice, equality, fraternity and unity in India, and in the face of the undeniable success of the democratic form of government in which all communities are equally represented, a revival of the partition of free India on a communal basis would certainly be disastrous. It might lead to civil war or to the extermination of many of the fifty-million Muslims living in all parts of India. Such might be the result of arousing the feelings of hatred which might flare up from such an unwise act. A moment's thought will make clear that the illegal and unjust claim of Pakistan to Kashmir and her intention of reviving communalism in India are things which do not fit in the contemporary age of science, technology, rockets and spaceships, which have reduced the human race to one family. The idea of establishing a theocratic state between Indian secular democracy on the one hand and the totalitarian Red Chinese regime on the other cannot be regarded as either realistic or rational. It becomes still more ridiculous when one appreciates that the cultural ties between India and Pakistan are unshakable. Culturally, lingually and geographically, West Pakistan is more akin to Northwestern India than to East Pakistan. When the Indians and Pakistanis meet each other in Western countries, they are spontaneously driven to feel this closeness, and in spite of apparent political differences meetings of individuals are like the meeting of brothers. At that moment the individuals feel that the political differences ought to disappear and they sincerely hope that India and Pakistan will stand should to shoulder in Asia. I have witnessed and experienced this feeling and spontaneous goodwill on more than one occasion in the U.S.A.

The point of mentioning this here is that India and Pakistan as two different sovereign democracies can be happiest and most prosperous when their cultural unity is recognized and when in the interest of the masses of both the countries political differences are bridged by mutual understanding. There were several instances of my meetings with Pakistan nationals in the U.S. during my stay in this country. In every instance we experienced the same closeness and affinity of culture. I therefore see no reason why India and Pakistan should not forget their political differences and unite morally to avert the common danger of Red Chinese imperialism which otherwise is likely to overpower both India and Pakistan.

There is need of true leadership in India as well as in Pakistan. Leaders of the caliber of Nehru, who can and who do actually hazard all for the promotion of freedom and the defense of democracy, can solve the problem of the rift between these two countries. The clear-headedness, the freedom from all religious and communal bias, the dedication to the cause of democracy and peace and the strong urge to see that a democratic economy delivers the goods to the average man were rare qualities of the personality and character of Mr. Jawahar Lal Nehru, Prime Minister of India. How his services and his political guidance helped India remain wedded to democracy and to reject totalitarianism will be the topic of the next chapter.

CHAPTER IX

The Leadership of Nehru

Not only first-hand shared political experience in attempting to solve some of the crucial problems of India, but certain democratically-inclined personalities have also strengthened the faith of Indians in the democratic way of life. Democracy presupposes leadership, and the success and failure of leadership, particularly in a new-born nation, weighs heavily in the balance of the success or failure of the nation concerned. If the leaders who become the torchbearers of the new nation are incapable, selfish, maneuvering and mean, they are bound either to reduce a democracy to a virtual dictatorship or to a political chaos which may bring about the displacement of democracy by totalitarianism. The attainment of political independence is the means to the promotion of individual freedom and the success of democracy. China was never subjugated by a foreign power as India was. She was not only politically free, but also had established a democratic government much earlier than India. But the democratic government deteriorated, living costs went up without a corresponding increase in per capita income, political chaos and frustration set in and ultimately violence and revolution spread over all China due largely to the failure of democratic leadership. Not only China, but countries like Cuba have undergone similar surgical operations resulting in the establishment of a Communistic regime because democratic leadership was lacking. No foreign aid, political device or advice can strengthen the morale of a country and infuse a conviction for democracy among its people if there is no national leadership of high caliber. Military coups in various Asian countries as well as in the West testify to the truth of the above statements. History properly understood is probably the best teacher of man, and if political leaders do not learn from history chaos and anarchy are almost certain to follow. Indian leaders have been wide awake ever since the commencement of their political struggle and they have at every step tried to learn from the history of other nations. Two political leaders of India, Gandhi and Nehru, whose greatness lay in learning from experience and open-mindedness, are chiefly responsible for the success and progress of democracy in India. Gandhi laid down the method and guided successfully the democratic struggle for independence. Nehru applied the Gandhian method to the internal and external policies of free India, keeping in view the goal of a modern democracy as economic prosperity and individual freedom in all spheres of life.

Lives of great men all over the world clearly show that greatness consists in an unselfish devotion to a general cause. Examples of such greatness in the West abound in the history of the nineteenth century. The names of Abraham Lincoln, Garibaldi, Livingstone and Louis Pasteur are worth mentioning in this connection. All these men were the embodiment of self-devotion, foresight, courage, and ceaseless efforts to serve mankind. India also produced such great men in the nineteenth century, among whom the names of Lakshmi Bai, the queen of Jhansi, Raja Ram Mohan Rou, Swami Dayananda, and Dada Bhai Narooji are worth mentioning. Lokmanya Tilak, the lion-hearted leader who preceeded Gandhi, and even Mahatma Gandhi himself, were in fact products of the nineteenth century in the sense that they attained their youth in the nineteenth century atmosphere. Gandhi, however, lived to serve the Indian nation and guide the political destinies of the country until January, 1948, and witnessed the dawn of independence himself. Nehru is the direct political successor of Gandhi and his thought has been greatly influenced by Gandhian philosophy and Gandhian ethics. Born into a wealthy family, Jawahar Lal Nehru nevertheless courted suffering, arrest and the trials and tribulations of jail life only to serve the general cause of the freedom of millions of his country men. Impressed by the sage, philosopher and compassionate seer Gandhi in his youth, a time which offered him the best possible opportunities for personally enjoying a luxurious life, Nehru gave up all the comforts of life voluntarily and joined the freedom struggle begun by Gandhi. His selfless devotion was evident in the fact that he chose to follow the strictly disciplined and rigorous life at the hermitage of Gandhi,

giving up all the comforts of his millionaire father's house, Anand
Bhavan (the "palace of joy"), and he did so when he was in the
prime of his youth. Although his father, Pandit Moti Lal Nehru,
had been converted to patriotism, and had become an acknowledged
national leader, his parental love towards Jawahar Lal prevented
him from seeing his son undergo the hardships of the disciplined
life of the Asharma (hermitage) of Gandhi. In spite of being educated in England from his childhood to youth, and in spite of
having become completely westernized so far as the comforts of
life were concerned, Jawahar Lal Nehru became a staunch follower
of Mahatma Gandhi and followed the rough and simple life of
the Gandhi Asharma to serve the cause of the teeming millions
of his country to achieve India's independence. Many stories are
popular in India with regard to the luxurious life of the Nehru
family prior to its joining the freedom movement. It is said, for
example, that Jawahar Lal's dresses were sent to Paris for dry
cleaning and washing. The fact remains that the Nehru family
plunged into the troubled waters of the struggle for independence
at great personal sacrifice. When young Nehru joined the Indian
National Congress no one believed there was the least possibility
of this party ever becoming the country's ruling party. On the
contrary, membership in this party meant inviting the wrath of
the British government, leading to criminal punishment and con-
fiscation of property.

One had to risk much in joining the Congress Party, which at
that time was an organization of bold workers prepared to court
jail and even death for the sake of freedom of the nation. The
ruling princes, wealthy capitalists, title holders and feudal lords
clung to the comforts and extraordinary privileges afforded them
by the British rulers. If the Nehru family had chosen to remain
neutral in India's struggle for independence, the British government might have showered further titles and grants of land upon
it and would have added to the wealth, splendor and glory of this
aristocratic family. Jawahar Lal Nehru's enthusiasm and patriotic
feeling made the whole family—father, mother, sisters and wife—
take the vow to fight for the independence of India at any cost.
The spirit of self-sacrifice not only on the part of Nehru but on the
part of his whole family is unique in the history of India and
perhaps in world history.

Pandit Moti Lal Nehru, the father of Shri Jawahar Lal Nehru, was a close associate of Mahatma Gandhi and had thrown in his lot with the new Congress movement started by Gandhi after the tragic massacre of Amritsar in 1919. He gave up a flourishing profession of law and underwent great financial loss. I have already referred to the incident of the Jallianwala Bagh in Amritsar. Shri Jawahar Lal Nehru himself was shocked when he came to know the details of this event. In his autobiography Shri Nehru Writes:

"Toward the end of the year (1919) I traveled from Amritsar to Delhi by the night train. The compartment I entered was almost full, and all the berths, except one upper one, were occupied by sleeping passengers. I took the vacant upper berth. In the morning I discovered that all my fellow passengers were military officers. They conversed with one another in loud voices, which I could not help overhearing. One of them was holding forth in an aggressive and triumphant tone, and soon I discovered that he was Dyer, the hero of Jallianwala Bagh, who was describing his Amritsar experiences. He pointed out how he had the whole town at his mercy and he had felt like reducing the rebellious city to a heap of ashes, but he took pity on it and refrained. He was evidently coming back from Lahore after giving his evidence before the Hunter committee of inquiry. I was greatly shocked to hear his conversation and to observe his callous manner." [1]

It was the Amritsar massacre and the results of the inquiry which inspired Pandit Moti Lal Nehru to throw himself into India's struggle for independence at any cost. Speaking of the conversation of his father Nehru wrote:

"The Punjab massacres and the inquiry into them had a profound effect on father. His whole legal and constitutional foundations were shaken by them, and his mind was gradually prepared for that change which was to come a year later." [2]

Ever since then the whole Nehru family devoted itself to the cause of Indian freedom, particularly in all the non-violent movements begun by Gandhi, offering satyagraha, going to jail and suffering all the consequences of separation, ill health, and death. Pandit Moti Lal Nehru died in harness, because in spite of ill-

---

[1] *Toward Freedom, The Autobiography of Jawahar Lal Nehru,* John Day company, 1962, p. 50.
[2] *Ibid.*

health he had courted arrests and imprisonment and devoted all his time and energy to the national work. During the civil disobedience campaign of 1930, all the adult members of the Nehru family volunteered and courted jail. Young and old were directly or indirectly serving the cause of India's freedom during the national unheaval. Not only did Pandit Moti Lal Nehru die in harness, but Kamala Nehru, Jawahar Lal's wife, also sacrificed her life. She herself went to jail and her health gradually deteriorated. It is worth mentioning how this truly great lady underwent suffering and continued to inspire Nehru through her spirit of self-sacrifice. Nehru's long absence from his family told upon Kamala's health, and reduced her to a mere skeleton. On an occasion when Kamala was seriously ill Nehru could watch over her only for eleven days, which was the interval between his two imprisonments. Describing her illness Nehru writes:

> "There she lay, frail and utterly weak, a shadow of herself, struggling feebly with the illness, and the thought she might leave me became intolerable. . . Our marriage had almost coincided with new developments in politics and absorption in them grew—so great became my concentration on these activities that, all unconsciously, I almost overlooked her and left her to her own resources, just when she required my full cooperation. My affection for her continued or even grew, and it was a great comfort to know that she was there to help me with her soothing influence. She gave me strength, but she must have suffered and felt a little neglected. An unkindness to her would almost have been better than this semiforgetful, casual attitude. . . And then came her recurring illness and my long absence in prison, when we could only meet at jail interviews. The civil disobedience movement brought her in the front rank of our fighters, and she rejoiced when she too went to prison. We grew ever nearer to each other. Our rare meetings became precious, and we looked forward to them and counted the days that intervened. . . Eighteen years of married life! But how many long years out of them had I spent in prison cells, and Kamala in hospitals and sanatoria? And now again I was serving a prison sentence and out just for a few days, and she was lying ill, struggling for life. I felt a little irritated at her for her carelessness about her health. And yet how could I blame her, for her eager spirit fretted at her inaction and her inability to take her full share in the national struggle? Physically unable to do so, she could neither take to work properly nor to treatment, and the fire inside her wore down the body." [1]

[1] *Ibid.*, p. 332-334.

Nehru was later transferred to Almora which was nearer Bhowali, where his wife had been brought for treatment. Prior to that, the British government had throughout kept him almost in the dark about the deteriorating condition of his wife. Attempts were made on the part of the government to coerce Nehru to get himself released from jail on his informal assurance to give up politics. He resisted the temptation although he knew that his presence by the bedside of his ailing wife could improve her condition. But his pledge to his country was dearer to him than his personal distress and the distress of his family. Nehru knew that even if he were to deviate from his ideal and obtain release from jail by giving assurances to remain aloof from politics, his wife would not approve. Kamala was throughout concerned with the cause of Indian independence and justice and she bravely faced all sufferings to enable her husband to serve the nation. This unique woman deserves the honor, admiration and gratitude of the Indian nation. Her little known service and sacrifice is unforgettable and most significant not only for Nehru but for India. I cannot help quoting Nehru himself with reference to this episode of Kamala's illness and her strong resolve to bear sufferings, disease and even death for the general cause.

> "Early in October I was taken to see her again. She was laying almost in a daze with a high temperature, she longed to have me by her, but, as I was leaving her to go back to prison, she smiled at me bravely and beckoned to me to bend down. When I did so, she whispered: 'What is this about your giving assurance to the Government? Do not give it'." [1]

Later on, Nehru was allowed once a month to visit ailing Kamala at Bhowali. However he was not released from jail. His wife had to go to Europe for further treatment, but Nehru remained in jail. This forced separation, which certainly had a shocking effect on Nehru before and after the death of his beloved wife, was probably the most pathetic episode in his life. He was released from jail only when the condition of his wife in Europe became most critical. He attended his wife during her last days and her death had a profound effect on his mind. Not only did Nehru lose his wife. His mother, who was shocked by the death of Kamala, soon after breathed her last. All this seemed to strengthen the character of Nehru who wrote:

---

[1] *Ibid.*, p. 337-8.

"Physically I am older, of course, but it is the mind that has received shock and sensation again and again and has hardened, or perhaps matured. My wife's death in Switzerland ended a chapter of my existence and took away much from my life that had been part of my being. It was difficult for me to realize that she was no more, and I could not adjust myself easily. I threw myself into my work, seeking more satisfaction in it, and rushed about from end to end of India. . . My mother's death later broke a final link with the past. My daughter was away studying at Oxford, and later under treatment in a sanitorium abroad. I would return to my home from wanderings almost unwillingly and sit in that deserted house all by myself trying even to avoid interviews there. I wanted peace after the crowds." [2]

Nehru was a man of crowds and he was at his best when he addressed huge gatherings. In spite of being educated entirely in England, and in spite of the fact that he thought and wrote in English, he spoke to the millions of Indians in simple and straightforward Hindustani, an amalgam of Hindi and Urdu. His speeches were inspiring and he had complete rapport with his audiences. A sincere and honest patriot, he was a strenuous worker, mentally quick and very intelligent, self-conscious though not self-conceited. These are some of the qualities for which he has been held in great esteem by the Indian people and loved even by his political opponents.

It goes without saying that every independent thinker, and more particularly a person who dedicates his life to a general cause, is bound to follow some fundamental principles which he accepts and endorses. Nehru relinquished comforts and embraced a hard life; he sacrificed his family happiness and his wealth for improving the lot of millions of his countrymen, for waging a constant and tough fight against British imperialism and for breaking the shackles of the slavery of a great but helpless country, which due to political vicissitudes had lost its ancient glory and its eminence as perhaps the most cultured and the most civilized nation of the world. His resolve to dedicate his life to the cause, his patriotic passion, his urge to free the ignorant and innocent millions from the clutches of hunger and penury, and his determination to achieve all this under the guidance of the great saint and philosopher, Mahatma Gandhi, makes it quite evident that what struck Jawahar

---

[2]*Ibid.*, p. 356.

Lal Nehru in his early years was not the hedonistic philosophy of life, but an altruistic spirit of self-sacrifice, restraint and active service in behalf of the suffering humanity of India.

Holding an extreme activistic philosophy of life it was not at all probable that Nehru would also be interested in the abstract questions of metaphysics. He himself agreed that "Some vague or more precise philosophy of life we all have, though most of us accept unthinkingly the general attitude of life which is the characteristic of our generation and environment." Nehru as an ethical thinker firmly believed in Gandhi's notion of the justification of means to justify ends. He has always admired the method of satyagraha, or truthful protest, for the attainment of freedom. "Freedom is the birthright of every individual", and the crushing of human freedom by the British imperialists in India was undoubtedly untruthful. Satyagraha, which also consisted in non-cooperation with the foreign government ruling millions of unwilling Indians, whose wealth had been exploited by the Britishers for centuries, was the most justified means for the just end of gaining political independence. Nehru emphasized the worthiness of the means both from the theoretical as well as from the practical point of view. In his autobiography he wrote: "A worthy end should have worthy means leading up to it. That seemed not only a good ethical doctrine but sound practical politics, for the means that are not good often defeat the end in view and raise new problems and difficulties." Nehru was concerned mainly, however, with the practical application of theories. He accepted the nobility of the means, the sincerity of purpose or "good will" as the best means, not merely because various thinkers and philosophers have put forward the intuitive theory of morality based on the intrinsic goodness of the good will, but because good results cannot possibly be achieved without the right means and the good will. He was essentially humanistic, and morality or the right for him was the means for the well being of humanity. For him nothing was more important than man, and hence man is an end in himself. But though a humanist Nehru always remained a utilitarian in the sense that he considered morality to be a means for the betterment of man and not an end in itself. A truly humanistic view, though moral, must essentially regard man—concrete man—to be the meeting ground of all values. Man generated the concept of value and value has meaning only for man. It is this humanistic attitude towards philosophy, ethics and religion which predominated in the thought of Nehru and prompted him to declare that "God we may deny, but what hope is there for us if we deny man and thus reduce everything to futility?" Indian philosophy from the early Vedic period has asserted the dignity of man and has declared him to be superior even to God because he is embodied Brahman. This attitude is present in Nehru's thought throughout and is responsible for his emphasis on improving the material lot of human beings.

Nehru's realism prompted him to adopt the humanistic approach to all problems and to subordinate all interests to the main interest of human wellbeing. Hence it was natural for him to be more a utilitarian than an intuitionist, to lay more emphasis on concrete consequences than on abstract motives. He was therefore not a mere speculator, but a practical thinker. He accepted the power of spirit, but this power according to him has been made active and effective because man has always put up a brave struggle against the odds of life. He says:

> "How amazing is this spirit of man. In spite of innumerable failings, man throughout the ages has sacrificed his life and all he held dear for an ideal, for truth, for faith, for country and honor. That ideal may change, but the capacity for self-sacrifice continues, and, because of that, much may be forgiven to man, and it is impossible to lose hope for man. In the midst of disaster, he has not lost his dignity or his faith in the values he cherished."

Nehru's faith in the self-sacrificing capacity of man, which in fact is the real "dignity" of man, was unshakable. If Kant was a moralist par excellence and so was Gandhi, Nehru can be rightly described as a humanist par excellence. He laid great emphasis on the human approach. He derided the absence of the human approach in science, although he admired sciences and the scientific method. Wherever he disagreed with the idealism of Gandhi or favored relative violence to absolute non-violence, he did so because of his extreme humanism.

Nehru was first and last a democrat and despised hero worship. There is no doubt that the people of India honored and almost worshipped Nehru, and had he the ambition to become dictator of India he could easily have achieved it. But, on the contrary, he has always tried to rid ignorant people of their slavish mentality. During the prime of his youth when he was elected president of the Indian National Congress he traveled almost all over India. Huge processions of millions of people showered flowers on him as he passed through the towns mounted on a horse. The spectacle aroused the patriotic feelings of the people and infused the spirit of self-sacrifice for the cause of India's freedom. But whenever a person reverently touched Nehru's feet out of ignorance, he would become annoyed and red with anger and even sometimes pushed the person back physically. He never allowed anyone to worship him as a superman. As the leader of the ruling party he many times made decisions against his personal likes and dislikes.

His democratic spirit revolted against autocratic tendencies. He gave vent to these feelings in an anonymous article published in an Indian journal, "Modern Review". In this article written about himself he warned the Indian people and politicians of the danger of dictatorship if he was over-eulogised. He wrote:

> "Men like Jawahar Lal, with all their great capacity for great and good work, are unsafe in a democracy. He calls himself a democrat, and socialist, and no doubt he does so in all earnestness . . . but a little twist and he might turn into a dictator. He might still use the language of democracy and socialism, but we all know fascism has fattened on this language and then cast it away as useless lumber." [1]

No leader of Nehru's status has ever been so self-analytical and self-critical, and his introspection on this score showed his strong desire to see India flourish. Since he was in the thick of active political life his interests and ambitions were bound to clash with the views of others. But on such occasions Nehru's preference for his own views were usually influenced by the general interest. He analyzed his own attitude and wrote that he should be subject to checks and balances. In the same anonymously written article he wrote:

> "Jawahar Lal cannot become a fascist. He is too much of an aristocrat for the cruelty and vulgarity of fascism. His very face and voice tell us that. His face and voice are definitely private. . . And yet he has all the makings of a dictator in him. . . vast popularity, a strong will, energy, pride . . . and with all his love of the crowd, an intolerance of others and a certain contempt for the weak and in-efficient. His flashes of temper are well known. His over-

---
[1] *Ibid.*, p. 437.

whelming desire to get things done, to sweep what he dislikes and build anew, will hardly prove for long the slow
process of democracy. . . His conceit is already formidable.
It must be checked. We want no Caesars."[1]

Nehru wrote this a year before India became independent and
before the responsibilities of the prime ministership fell on his
shoulders. There is little doubt that many of the traits of his
character mentioned above played an important role in his contribution towards the building of free India.

The dominant passion of Nehru was to see India prosper and
make unprecedented social, political and economic progress in the
shortest possible time. If it were within his powers he would have
liked to see every village of India not only electrified and in-
dustralized, but also equipped with nuclear power for agriculture
and automation. But, unfortunatly, India is far behind in technology and scientific research. She needs economic aid and special-
ized training. Her industry, which has taken long strides during
the past decade and a half, still needs to be accelerated, as we
have seen. It is therefore necessary for India to base her foreign
policy on firm and realistic grounds. Nehru made a great contribution to the building of the Indian nation by guiding her
foreign policy with reference to her economic development. No
new nation can flourish entirely on the capital of a foreign nation; nor can she flourish if she remains isolated from other progressive nations. Keeping in view these facts Nehru adopted what
has come to be known as the policy of "non-alignment" so far as
military alliances with the Western bloc or the Russian bloc were
concerned. We will discuss this aspect of Nehru's contribution
towards the strengthening of Indian democracy in the sequel.

----

[1]Ibid.

CHAPTER X

India after Jawahar Lal Nehru

We have seen how Nehru emerged to lead the newly born democracy and how he devoted himself wholeheartedly to the cause of the nation. He lived for the sake of his country and died as a result of the intolerable personal suffering stimulated by the wantonness of a neighboring country towards a land of peace, love and nonviolence, ideals ever cherished and practiced by Nehru. He could not tolerate Red China's stabbing India in the back and ultimately he could not survive the shock. He had never imagined that after the friendly attitude of India toward China, after India's honest support of Red China's membership in the United Nations (even at the cost of being misunderstood by the friendly democracies), and finally after the signing of the covenant of "Peaceful Coexistence" that the Communists would exploit India's complacency and resort to an undeclared unilateral war. Chinese leaders took advantage of India's good will for India had trusted the pseudo peace-promoting demonstrations of China, manifest particularly in the much advertised "Peaceful Coexistence" document. Nehru had for a time tolerated the "Rape of Tibet" and even swallowed the insults administered by Chinese leaders on several occasions of his sympathetic statements in support of the Tibetans. But when on humanitarian grounds he rightly gave refuge to the deposed Tibetan head and his followers, who escaped to India, the fuming and fretting of the Maoists became an unbearable trial to Nehru. Yet even then he believed that some day good sense would prevail among the Red Chinese.

Not only Red China's aggression, which was intended to take advantage of India's unpreparedness for any kind of confrontation in modern warfare, but also the unexpected silence of Russia during the critical hour when India's fate hung in the balance had an untoward effect on Nehru's mind. I presume that he felt that Russia's publicly announced appreciation of India's nonalignment policy, which India had formally taken as genuine admiration, was perhaps more lip service than sincere sympathy for the developing Indian democracy. It is true that Russia had long since developed its ideological rift with China, and it had become obvious that Kruschev could not possibly exert any moral or political pressure to dissuade Red China from attacking the "Friend" of the Soviet Union and a supporter of Red China's admission to the U.N. But it was difficult to judge the intention of this grim silence. Russia expressed her helplessness by saying that her predicament was that of being between the devil and the deep sea because one of the combatants was her "Brother" and the other was (just) a "Friend". This vague but strategically diplomatic explanation did not solve the mystery and attitude of the Russian leaders, especially the delay in Russia's delivery of certain aircraft which were expected for India's self-defense much earlier than the Chinese aggression. Nehru must have realised at that moment that the policy of nonalignment, however laudable, was not realistic. He announced that he had been "disillusioned" although he did not say whether his disillusionment was with reference to Red China or to the whole complicated situation.

But nevertheless it was wise not to give up India's nonalignment policy in spite of unprecedented material and practical hardships which the nation had to face at that time. Perhaps the western democracies, and particularly the United States, discerned Nehru's predicament. Subsequent arms aid from both the United States and the United Kingdom gave Nehru courage. But the situation did reveal the bitter fact that if India was determined to maintain her nonaligned status she would have to be militarily strong and self-sufficient. But how could self-sufficiency in defense be achieved in a single day after an idealistic complacency of a decade and a half? That was the puzzling and frustrating problem facing the Indian leader.

Nehru had robust health. He was agile, alert, and dynamic. He seldom rested, sleeping only for short intervals. His secretaries worked all hours of the day and night, for Nehru frequently dictated until past midnight. But owing to his regular habits and physical exercise he always appeared fresh and healthy. I remember my last meeting with him on December 28, 1961. A few months before Red China's aggression against India I had been granted an interview to present the Prime Minister the first copy of my book, *A Critical Study of Western Ethics.* I had dedicated this book to Mr. Nehru. After breakfast Mr. Nehru appeared in his drawing room where several visitors were waiting. I was the first to be presented to him. Mr. Nehru recognized me owing to previous meetings, and greeted me with a smile, saying, "Oh, you are here again!" I paid my respects to him in the traditional Indian fashion with folded hands and presented him my book. He patted me on the shoulder and said, "You are doing good work. Go on working, young man. India needs real hardworking people." I thanked him for his encouragement and then introduced my student, Miss Rukmani Bhati, a nineteen year old princess of Rajasthan, who was then studying for her master's degree in Philosophy. Much against the wishes of many royal families of other princely states this young lady cast off her purdah, enrolled in college for graduate studies, became a "commoner" and mixed with all kinds of students. When I told this to Mr. Nehru he seemed very pleased. He talked to the princess for several minutes as she told him her aims and what she was studying. He expressed admiration for her courage and advised her to complete her studies.* As Mr. Nehru talked there was a glow on his face. He appeared healthy and cheerful in spite of being weighed down with the administration and public affairs of the largest democracy in the world. I remained with him as he talked to his other visitors. Most of them had come to pay their respects. I noticed the soundness of his judgement and his firmness of mind. In that connection I would like to mention an episode that took place then.

One of his visitors was an old acquaintance. He had apparently come to pay his respects, but as it turned out he had in fact intended to try to persuade Mr. Nehru to alter a decision of the local political unit of his native town which did not favor his candidacy for the Congress Party ticket in the next general election.

---

*It may not be out of place to mention here that this young woman did get her Master's degree in 1962 and was married to a prince of the state of Rajpipla near Bombay. Her colorful marriage was celebrated in Jaisalmer where her father and grandfather had ruled prior to this state's merger with India. The story of this marriage with color pictures was reported in the *National Geographic Magazine,* January, 1965.

He tried to impress upon Mr. Nehru that he was superior to a female candidate sponsored by his local Congress Committee, and he
reminded Mr. Nehru of his valuable past service to the organization, some of which had been personally known to the "beloved
Prime Minister" (these were the words he used). But in spite of
the fact that Mr. Nehru knew his past record, and in spite of a
possible temptation to favor an old colleague, he did not agree.
On the contrary he argued forcefully with the visitor and finally
convinced him that it was best under the circumstances that the
candidate submit to the decision of the local Congress Committee
as a devoted party worker. I believe this interview is some evidence
of how sound and mentally alert Nehru was just a few months
before the calamity of the Red Chinese attack.

With regard to his quickness and agility, I would also like to
mention how on that same morning Nehru completed his appointment with six hundred students who had come to meet him and
to be photographed with him, and how he pushed out of his
drawing room to reach his appointment on time. The students,
who had been waiting for him on the vast lawns of the Prime
Minister's residence, eagerly watched him approach from the porch
accompanied by his secretaries, bodyguards and some of the visitors,
including myself and Miss Bhati, and they were sitting in different
groups. Just before the photographs were taken, Mr. Nehru was
expected to address these students who had come on an educational
tour from distant towns. He spoke inspiringly for a few minutes;
he always loved to open his heart to the youth of India. He exhorted them to keep their eyes wide open, and to follow the example
of the developed nations and to be prepared to defend Indian
democracy at all costs. After the speech he literally ran, jumping
from one group of students to another, fulfilling the desires of all
the students to be photographed with him. Quickly he would jump
from one group to the other, motion the photographer to follow,
sit in the center, get himself and the students photographed and
dash to the next group. At the same time he was laughing, making
jokes with the students and playing pranks. The reader can imagine
how pleased and gratified the students were at that moment. Nehru
was the man of the masses and he always identified himself with
the masses. Often disregarding security measures he would walk
into the crowds in public meetings to mingle with the people.
Once his bodyguards had to lift him bodily when he mixed with a

crowd, in spite of his reluctance to be so guarded. To return to the events of that morning: he said goodbye to the students, turned around and rushed towards the porch where his car was waiting. It was just a few minutes before nine and he wanted to reach his office on time: He approached the car, snatched the wallet of his lunch and a flask of tea which one of his attendants had been holding and very smartly jumped into his seat. Bidding goodbye to all the visitors surrounding him, in a moment he was off. I have mentioned all this to suggest that his end was brought about mainly by the severe mental shock which he endured as a direct result of the Chinese invasion, and not by an ordinary failure of bodily functions.

Nehru was also pained when he heard about the tragic death of Mr. Kennedy, who had been a great admirer of Nehru and whose far-sighted policy had been responsible for military aid to India at a most critical moment of the Chinese aggression. This gesture had given great consolation to Nehru. Thus the death of President Kennedy was most unexpected and most shocking for an already shaken Prime Minister. From all these causes his body gave way and his heart weakened. A few weeks after President Kennedy's passing, Nehru suffered a severe heart attack and gradually became weaker and weaker. In spite of the finest medical attention he could not regain his health and he passed away in the last week of May, 1964. "The light was out", and the entire nation was plunged into unprecedented mourning. Huge crowds thronged around the Prime Minister's residence and within a few hours millions of mourners became a human sea. In spite of great precautions to control the crowds several persons were crushed to death. Every one was anxious to pay homage to the mortal remains of the great and venerated leader, beloved of the young and old, the darling "uncle" of millions of Indian children. A devoted patriot, a selfless and honest statesman, a lover of the peasant and the laborer, an admirer of the youth and a relentless worker, his like would perhaps never be born again in India. In his will, which he had executed and sealed more than a decade before his death, he expressed the desire that after the cremation of his remains the ashes should be scattered over the fields of India where the farmer and the laborer worked. He wished his ashes to be literally mingled with the physical body of his motherland. Such was Jawahar (the first name of Nehru), which literally means "gem", and such were his feelings for his country and his fellowmen.

Possessed of these outstanding qualities and taking into account the unstinted faith of the people of India in him it was natural that Nehru outshone every one else. He loved his people and they loved him with even greater intensity. His mere presence attracted millions of men and women of all ages, and different communities and faiths to walk long distances merely to catch a glimpse of their beloved leader. They thought that by "having the Darshan" (seeing with reverence) of this divine person they would be blessed and purified. Millions of illiterates took his word to be the word of God, although Nehru abhorred the idea of being idolised. Yet in many respects Nehru was India and India was Nehru. Even in the international field it was only Nehru who was recognized as a world figure after Gandhi's death. He was in all minds one of the greatest living personalities of the world in our century. Such greatness has of course its serious disadvantages. Probably the greatest disadvantage of an outstanding leader and the nation which he leads, especially if the nation is newly born, is to face the problem of choosing his successor. This was the predicament of the Indian nation after the demise of the Prime Minister, who was a God to the illiterate masses, a deeply respected leader of the politicians, including the opposition, an inspirer of intellectuals and educators of all shades of opinion, a sincere friend to the youth and a loving "uncle" to the children of India.

As pointed out previously, Nehru had not chosen a successor because in his view it would have been undemocratic to do so. But he did think that the successful candidate ought to possess humility, self-devotion and a unique balance. As we shall see later such a leader was elected unanimously, setting at naught all gloomy speculations of the prophets of doom. How did it come about and why? In order to explain this we must note a few vital changes within the affairs of the Congress Party which were most timely and effective for the solidarity of that secular party and for the unity of the whole nation. Just before Nehru became ill, and just after the passing of the Red Chinese menace, the Congress Party decided to utilise the talents of its leaders both in its organizational and administrative wings. This was known as the "Kamaraj Plan", one of the chief purposes of which this was to bring about a change of persons who had repeatedly been coming to political power term after term.

A few more words about the christening of this measure of political reform, the "Kamaraj Plan", seem necessary especially for western readers who may not be familiar with political developments in India. The Congress Party has always had within its fold many selfless workers and leaders whose lives are dedicated to the service of the party. Mr. Kamaraj Nadar, popularly known as "Kamaraj", is one of those stalwarts of the Congress Party of whom not only this particular organization but the whole of India can genuinely be proud. He dedicated his life to the cause of freedom, espoused by the Congress Party from its inception, and gained great popularity in his native state of Madras. He attained the highest possible office as Chief Minister in his state, which is well-reputed for the high level of education amongst its inhabitants and which has produced top-ranking intellectuals, scientists, politicians and philosophers. Shri Rajgopal Achari, who was the first Indian Governor General, and whose farsightedness in politics was once unquestioned, also comes from this state; he chose to serve as Chief Minister of Madras even after he had retired as Governor General of India, the highest position in the country. Mr. Kamaraj is not acquainted with English nor with Hindi, the national language of India. He does not know any language other than Tamil, the native language of his state. Even so he was elected Chief Minister of Madras because of his extraordinary intelligence, integrity, selfless devotion and strength of character. He has a sharp mind and a very strong will. It was he who proposed that all office-holders in the administrative wing of the Congress Party submit their resignations to a selected committee and volunteer to accept duties allotted to them either in the administrative wing or in the organizational wing as the said committee decided in the interest of rejuvenating the party. Kamaraj's plan was a novel and revolutionary one, but it was adopted by the Congress Party in 1963. It was a wise step. The lure of political power was largely responsible for neglect of the ideals of this national organization on the part of many veteran Congress leaders who could render better service to the organization and to fostering the secular and national ideology of the party among the masses than in running the administration. Moreover, this plan would also minimise the evils of one party rule in the Indian democracy.

Statesmen and politicians throughout the world were interested in the outcome of Mr. Kamaraj's efforts to get a unanimous vote for the candidate to succeed Nehru. When the decision was announced in favor of Lal Bahadur Shastri, politicians of every shade and opinion welcomed it, intellectuals honored it, and the common man rejoiced at it. The only other candidate, who had for some time resisted withdrawing his name from the contest, was Mr. Morarji Desai, a farmer, Minister of Finance and a senior member of the Congress Party. But ultimately not only did he withdraw his name but proposed the name of Mr. Lal Bahadur Shastri for Prime Minister in the official meeting of the Congress Parliamentary Committee. This decision was applauded by all because Mr. Shastri was the only person acceptable even to the opposition parties. He had grown to his stature gradually because of his steady and sincere work right from the level of a volunteer party worker to that of Cabinet Minister of the highest rank. Here was an example of a man who moved from the humble hut to the Prime Minister's Palace or, in the American idiom, 'from log cabin to the White House.'

Almost all foreign governments which had diplomatic relations with India congratulated Dr. Radhakrishnan, the President of India. Although it was a surprise to many Western statesmen that India had tided over a crisis, many mature observers of Indian politics had taken Mr. Shastri's election for granted. It is in this connection that the Kamaraj Plan played a vital part in maintaining unity in the Congress ranks and in making the historic decision of Mr. Shastri's election a unique national and international event. Mr. Shastri had resigned under the Kamaraj Plan and was no longer a Cabinet Minister. But when Mr. Nehru fell ill and wanted a trusted assistant who could carry on his policies and lighten the burden of his work, Mr. Shastri was requested to join the Central Cabinet as Minister without Portfolio. Since the request came from the top, and since Mr. Shastri never opposed the wishes of Mr. Nehru, he accepted the office. Thus he was virtually initiated as the prospective successor of Nehru. Many leading Congressmen felt this and therefore they were not surprised by the unanimous election of Mr. Shastri.

There is no doubt about Mr. Morarji Desai's many fine qualities, but somehow he was not acceptable to many sections of the Parliament and the general public. Mr. Desai had become unpopular as a Finance Minister chiefly on account of his influence in getting the Gold Control Bill passed in Parliament. But opposition to him was based largely on misunderstanding. This measure proposed by Mr. Desai was in the national interest and was welcomed by the economists. Mr. Desai faced the opposition to his bill resolutely and courageously. As a man of strong will he would not compromise on this and many other issues concerning Congress ideology. He is a staunch follower of Mahatma Gandhi and an incorrigible advocate of total prohibition. These are laudable qualities in this veteran Congress leader. What stood in his way was an uncompromising nature sometimes amounting to intolerance and obstinacy. However, in a democracy plasticity and toleration or respect for the opinions of others are necessary ingredients for successful leadership. What secured unanimous support for Mr. Lal Bahadur Shastri were his humility, his unassuming nature, his selflessness and an absence of ostentation and self-assertion of any kind.

Mr. Shastri's outward softness was combined with a strong determination to lead his nation to the path of progress and prosperity. He was in the habit of taking his time in deciding vital matters but his decisions were firm and irrevocable. In some internal matters he was perhaps more successful than Nehru. He took strong measures to root out corruption among the ministers and was courageous enough to dismiss one very strong Chief Minister of a border State as a result of a public inquiry conducted by an ex-Supreme Court judge. Although this judge had begun his inquiry while Mr. Nehru was living, the report was submitted after Mr. Shastri assumed the office of Prime Minister. Mr. Shastri immediately executed the findings of the record and replaced the Chief Minister without any loss of time. The people of that state had been under the impression that the high-handed Chief Minister had been spared because all the facts could not reach Mr. Nehru, although this impression is not correct. Mr. Nehru himself had instituted the inquiry after a regular procedure. But since it was the privilege of Mr. Shastri to execute the decision and since he did not delay removing the Chief Minister, most people concluded that Mr. Shastri had accomplished something which even Mr. Nehru could not.

Mr. Shastri had to face many complicated problems during his short term in office. The first of these was the issue of the national language. This problem, of course, was not his own creation but an inherited issue which dated back to the nineteen thirties when the All-India Congress Session had unanimously passed a resolution that after the attainment of independence Hindi should be made the national language of India. When India became independent the Constituent Assembly drafted the Constitution of India, and a resolution was incorporated in it stating that Hindi would replace English as the coordinating official language at the center and between the states. It was further stated that the different regional languages would remain the official languages for different states. This constitutional step was necessary both for the development of the regional languages, which had been neglected by the British government, and also for the emotional integration of the multi-cultural and multi-lingual character of the vast country of India. The Constitution was unanimously adopted by the Indian Parliament on January 26, 1950, and it was resolved that this lingual change would be effected after an interval of fifteen years, that is, on January 26, 1965. Not a single voice was raised against this constitutional measure at that time. The interval was necessary to make the change gradual and convenient for preparing the people to learn Hindi. As a matter of fact even the regional languages had to be developed because they were to become the official languages of different states. Only two per cent of the people of India know English. It was of course picked up by the Indians under the pressure of the British because it had been made the official language of the entire country. As a result of this neither Hindi, which is understood by at least forty per cent of the people of India, nor the regional languages had any official status whatsoever. Since after independence one of the indigenous languages was to become the national and official language Hindi was selected, but the adoption of Hindi as the federal language necessarily involved the automatic development of the other regional languages which would simultaneously be given status as official languages in the various states.

It is true that preparations for the changeover had not been carried out efficiently, nor had the fact of the need for developing regional languages as official media of the business of State administration been made known throughout the country. It fell to the lot of Mr. Shastri's administration to bring about the change by the deadline set by the Parliament in 1950. Although the fifteen year interval had been given for the benefit of the people and particularly for central government employees, this time lag proved to be detrimental to the whole issue. Had no time limit been set at the beginning, and had the learning of Hindi (as well as the regional languages) been introduced and developed after the adoption of the language clause of the Constitution, it would have been possible to carry out the measure without opposition. During the interval of fifteen years many political parties used the opportunity to generate controversy and they aroused regional sentiments among the innocent masses. One particular political party, known as Dravida Munetra Kazgham, which is mainly confined to the Tamil-speaking area of the south, excluding the States of Kerala and Andhra, carried on many subversive activities which were detrimental to national unity and emotional integration. The followers of this party (mistakenly) claimed that the adoption of Hindi as a national language would be detrimental to the regional language of Madras State. This was just the opposite of the purpose of the changeover. On the contrary, the regional language of Madras, called Tamil, could not be the official language of the State as long as the changeover was not adopted and as long as the British-imposed English language remained the official language at the center and in the states. It was due to this misunderstanding that the State of Madras opposed the changeover. As a result misguided violent demonstrations and self-immolations took place in that area. There were no counter-demonstrations on the part of the Hindi-speaking states or those which supported the change in spite of being non-Hindi-speaking areas. It is worth mentioning here that three out of four persons who committed immolation did not know the English language. This suggests that they did not understand that they were burning themselves to death for retaining *that* language as the national language of India, which they did not know themselves.

The facts reveal that the whole movement was misconstrued and misguided. If the central government had taken drastic steps to crush the demonstrations, there could have been the possibility of aggravating an already delicate and explosive situation. But Mr. Shastri dealt with the matter calmly, courageously and patiently. A convention of the Chief Ministers of all the States was held at New Delhi, and it was resolved that English as well as Hindi should remain the coordinating languages for some time to come. In other words, when the English-knowing generation retired from the central service and the Hindi-knowing generations took charge of administration, the problem of the national language would automatically be solved.

The second and the third knotty problems which Mr. Shastri had to face were those of the border issue of the Rann of Kutch and the Kashmir issue, both of which are linked. I will therefore deal with both these problems under one heading, namely, "Indo-Pakistan Hostilities." I have already explained how Pakistan's attitude of hatred and religious fanaticism, which is opposed to the secular policy of Indian democracy, has been responsible for the unnecessary differences between the sovereign nations of India and Pakistan. At first, Pakistan made an unprovoked attack on an area known as the Rann of Kutch in northwest India and occupied a territory which she claimed to be her own. Mr. Shastri showed great patience and restraint at the time of this crisis. He did not adopt the policy of an eye for an eye. He preferred to watch and wait and was criticised as slow and sluggish by some of his own countrymen. Finally, he succeeded in bringing Pakistan from the battlefield to the table. Although it was a step towards future understanding between India and Pakistan, and although Mr. Shastri had been motivated only by good will, the Pakistan leaders continued their old practice of arousing the violently national sentiments of their own people and of maintaining the war psychology which they always considered conducive to grabbing and maintaining power in the theocratic state of Pakistan. The peaceful moves of the Indian Prime Minister were misconstrued as cowardice by the Pakistan authorities with the result that secret preparations for an armed attack on India were immensely increased.

As a result, five thousand Pakistanis (trained largely by the Red Chinese) were infiltrated into the Kashmir area of Indian territory with a view to sabotage, and Pakistan's regular forces were made ready to attack. The date for this attack was set as August 8, 1965. But the Indian government came to know of the plan on August 5 and began searching and clearing the areas of the infiltrators. This certainly postponed the major attack of Pakistan on India for at least a month. On the 5th of September Pakistan crossed the boundary line and advanced scores of miles into the Indian territory in the Poonchh area. It became unavoidable for India to defend herself by resorting to arms and by paying the aggressor in the same coin. The conflict changed into an open war and Pakistan counted on the strength of her superior arms, Sabre jets and Patton tanks which had been supplied her generously under the SEATO and CENTO agreements to be used for her defense against possible Red aggression. Pakistan, as I have already indicated, had always dreamt of conquering India by force, and her act of joining SEATO and CENTO was from the very beginning motivated by this ambition. When during the Red Chinese attack Pakistan made open declarations against India and sang the praises of Red China as the saviour of Asia it was quite evident that this fanatic theocratic state under its dictatorially motivated leaders would go to any length to fulfill this ambition. That was my observation three years ago although this chapter is being added to the manuscript in 1966. There is no doubt that such an ambition is an empty dream, but the Pakistani leaders have always fed their masses on the propaganda of hatred against India and on the slogans that they must occupy any territory which Muslims inhabit. This Nazi spirit of Pakistan appeared in naked form during this hot war waged by Pakistan under the impression that India would not resist, or not resist effectively. Indian forces, in spite of being handicapped by their inferior and to some extent outmoded arms, were imbued with the spirit of patriotism. They went to great lengths to defend their freedom and were able to meet the violent challenge of Pakistan so successfully that they even downed Sabre jets with their home made small fighters called Gnats and smashed the "invincible" Patton tanks. The nation was united. Indian Muslims fought for the freedom of India vigorously. It is worth mentioning here that the soldier who was given the highest military honor for smashing the largest number of Pakistani tanks single-handed was a Muslim of India, Hamid Khan. This suggests that arms and slogans do not build a nation nor does religious fanaticism mean democracy. India's faith in democracy and secularism was strengthened all the more by this war, and the response of all the communities, including the Muslim community, gave a new dimension to Indian nationalism.

Pakistan transgressed international laws of warfare and bombarded many civilian areas causing untold loss of life and property. But fortunately for India ninety-five percent of the Pakistani air strikes were miscalculated and misfired. Many one-thousand-pound bombs fell unexploded on soft ground. Some bombs did not explode even on the hard ground in the heart of the border city of Jodhpur in Rajasthan. In this town a dangerously amusing event occurred. One of the one-thousand-pound bombs hurled by the Pakistan Air Force fell on a roadside in a village in the vicinity of Jodhpur during the night raid. It remained unexploded and was discovered by an illiterate peasant who was driving his bullock cart to another village. He had never seen a bomb in his life and was fascinated by this huge cylindrical object lying on the roadside unclaimed. He thought that perhaps it was some valuable piece of machinery which might have dropped from some truck carrying goods from town to town. He wanted to lift it up, put it in his cart and deposit it in the lost property department of the district administrator's office. Unable to do the job by himself he called on a few persons living in the vicinity and they helped him to load the object in his cart. He carried it for more than twenty miles to the collectorate. The collector and other officers were both amused and horrified at the innocent bravery and honesty of the farmer. It was later detonated safely. Such incidents and many stories of the bravery of Indian soldiers strengthened the morale of the masses of India and few moved from the border areas in spite of their exposure to air raids. Lal Bahadur Shastri, who had agreed with the military in giving up passive resistance and in replying to the aggressor strategically, was hailed as a hero and a courageous political leader. There is little doubt that the objective of the Indian army was very limited, but it had to be strategic and efficient owing to the small quantity and poor quality of Indian arms. India had been manufacturing eighty-percent of her war material herself with a view to preparing for another Red Chinese attack and her preparedness for the Chinese menace was indeed tested in this conflict. When hundreds of Pakistan's Patton tanks were either destroyed or crippled and abandoned, and when three-fourths of her military strength had been used up and wasted, Pakistan's leaders agreed to the cease-fire with a view to save their face before their own public since they could not lead their nation to the promised land of Kashmir and New Delhi, the capital of secular India.

India had always insisted on peaceful settlement of all disputes and she always welcomed any move for a cease-fire. Even when the Security Council passed the cease-fire resolution on December 20, 1965, India was the first to accept it unconditionally, although materially India, and not Pakistan, the aggressor, had been victorious in the conflict. It was discovered later that whereas Pakistan had been able to conquer 250 square miles of Indian territory, India took over 750 square miles of Pakistan. They could have occupied more, but they did not advance, because India never had nor has, the ambition of conquering or destroying Pakistan. India wants Pakistan to flourish as a neighboring free nation, whatever its administrative structure might be. It is in the interest of both of these countries, in the interest of all the developing nations of Asia and Africa and in the interest of the free democracies of the whole world that Indo-Pakistan relations should be as cordial as those between the United States and Canada. Mr. Shastri, who represented the feelings of the whole nation, not only welcomed the cease-fire but was almost overanxious to have a long-term peace treaty with Pakistan. Red China, which had threatened India during this conflict more than once, advised Pakistan secretly not to enter into any such treaty. But it appears that Russia was very keen to see peace established in the Indian subcontinent. So the Russian Premier, Mr. Kosygin, invited the heads of the state of India and Pakistan to Tashkent for the possibility of a long term peace treaty on such honorable terms as were acceptable both to India and Pakistan. But just before this meeting between Shastri and Ayub Khan was scheduled, Khan, whose supporters and whose tutored public had been abusing the United States as an imperialistic nation, and had been burning images of Mr. Johnson during the days of the conflict between India and Pakistan, paid a hurried visit to the United States. The purpose of his visit was to re-establish "cordial relations", to make amends for the attack on the U.S. library in Karachi, to atone for the secret collusion of Pakistan with Red China and to prepare the ground for the resumption of military aid to his country. The disillusioned President of the United States, Lyndon Johnson, dealt with him cordially but realistically and made it quite clear that the settlement of the disputes with India could be possible in the ensuing Tashkent meeting and through the United Nations' good offices. It was made clear to Ayub Khan that the establishment of peace on the subcontinent of India and Pakistan was imperative. I think this was the most positive contribution Mr. Johnson made to the cause of peace and freedom in Southeast Asia. He and his advisors realised that armed conflict between India and Pakistan would help only

Red China, whose whole purpose was to weaken both India and Pakistan economically as well as militarily in order to "liberate" the whole of Asia under the banner of "Maoism".

This realistic attitude of the President of the United States had a sobering effect on the President of Pakistan. As a result the Tashkent meeting, which was personally attended by Mr. Shastri accompanied by many of his important colleagues, did succeed in the long run. In spite of many major disagreements between the Indian and Pakistani viewpoints at that historic meeting, and in spite of the fact that most of the observers were pessimistic about the outcome, the scenes in Tashkent changed from hopelessness to hopefulness, from hopefulness to rejoicing at the success of the final agreement, and finally to a mixed feeling of joy and sorrow at the sudden death of Mr. Shastri, the hero of the peace who had played a very important role of tolerance, patience and courage during all the talks at the meeting which turned out to be his last. Shastri's body was lifted by Mr. Ayub Khan and Mr. Kosygin before it was placed in the aircraft that brought his remains to New Delhi. Millions of men, women, children, young and old paid a homage of heartfelt condolence to this unique leader who within a short period of eighteen months had attained great popularity and enjoyed the endearment of his countrymen. This was the second major tragedy faced by the Indian nation within a year and a half. People had not yet been free from the grief of Nehru's death when Mr. Shastri also passed away. His mission was over. By his personal example Mr. Shastri may have proved that an ideal Indian must risk his life for the maintenance of peace and the protection of freedom and democracy. He surely strengthened the faith of the people of India in the democratic way of life.

This unexpected end of a brilliant political career once again created the problem of the selection of a suitable leader for the Congress Party. During his tenure Mr. Shastri was readily accepted by all as the country's leader, including persons who had opposed him on many issues. He had even consulted the members of opposition parties in vital and urgent matters concerning the destiny of the nation. He would hear all opinions and draw his own conclusions. The last decision that he had taken was that of signing the Tashkent treaty which he said was the beginning and not the end of the efforts to bring lasting peace to the subcontinent of India and Pakistan. The Tashkent agreement covered a vast field and stipulated that both India and Pakistan would never resort to war for any mutual dispute, including the dispute over territory. Not only this but both nations agreed that neither would indulge in any propaganda or publicity which might jeopardize the cordial relations between them.

It was therefore necessary that the next Prime Minister of India be a person who could successfully carry on the policies of Nehru and Shastri and also be sufficiently trained both in national and the international politics. The country now needed an honest, patriotic and energetic Prime Minister to solve its internal problems and also to carry out effectively the commitment of nonalignment in the international field. It was also necessary that the future Prime Minister appeal to Congressmen as well as to the general public. All these qualities were noticeable in the personality of Mrs. Indira Gandhi, the brilliant daughter of the brilliant father, Mr. Nehru. Who else could be more capable of running the administration of the young democracy of India than the person who from her early childhood had been brought up in an atmosphere of patriotism, selfless devotion and self-sacrifice?

I have already mentioned how the Nehru family sacrificed all comforts and domestic tranquillity for the sake of the whole nation. When Indira was only three years old, her family was in the thick of India's politics. Her father as well as her grandfather were staunch supporters of Gandhi, the "father" of the Indian nation. Mahatma Gandhi's ideals influenced all the members of the Nehru family. Many political meetings of the Indian National Congress Party used to be held at "Ananda Bhavan", the residence of the Nehrus. Many times young Indira experienced the cruel treatment of the British government, which snatched away her parents and her grandfather for long intervals and sent them to prison. This strengthened her faith in the service of her nation and, as we shall see, these impressions of early childhood made her a hardened soldier of the national party. Indira's childhood indicated a patriotic tendency, which was further fostered by her father's letters from jail. These letters have been published in the form of a book, *Letters From Father to Daughter,* and have been widely read with great interest. In one of the letters Nehru reminded the young Indira not to forget the example of Joan of Arc whose account had fascinated her when she first studied it. He wrote: "Do you remember how fascinated you were, when you first read the story of Joan of Arc and how your ambition was to be something like her? In India today we are making history, and you and I are fortunate to see this happening before our eyes. I cannot say what part will fall to our lot, but whatever it be, let us remember that we can do nothing that may bring discredit on our cause or dishonor to our people. Goodbye, little one, and may you grow up a brave soldier in India's service."

There is no doubt that she did grow up to be a courageous soldier and devoted her time and energies by turns to the cause of the Indian National Congress and to the management her father's household. She sacrificed her own comforts and attended to the creative work which she was able to do in various capacities in the Congress Party. She rose to the position of the President of the Congress Party and during her tenure was able to infuse new enthusiasm into its program. When Mr. Nehru was alive she probably deserved to hold the position of a minister or of an ambassador, but Mr. Nehru never wanted this to happen because it would have raised suspicions with regard to his fairness, which was a fond and special characteristic of Nehru. I rather feel that not to have given a chance to Indira Gandhi to become a first-rate leader during the lifetime of Mr. Nehru, though laudable from the point of view of integrity, was a kind of injustice. There is no doubt that Mrs. Gandhi possessed the talents, aptitudes and experience which, combined with her youthful energy, would enable her to hold any responsible office when Mr. Nehru was Prime Minister. Simply because she happened to be the daughter of the then head of state should not have stood in the way of obtaining her a deserving position which she could have otherwise been given. Undue favor toward relatives is no doubt nepotism. But so is undue disfavor, for both of them involve injustice. There are examples in other leading democracies in the West where deserving kith and kin of the head of the state have been entrusted with high political positions on merit. The son-in-law of Winston Churchill held an office during the Prime Ministership of his father-in-law. Similarly, the late U. S. President Kennedy was bold enough to appoint his brother, Mr. Robert Kennedy, as Attorney General of the United States. Few deny his competence in directing that office. I therefore feel that depriving Mrs. Gandhi of high office in the cabinet was overdoing justice. Nevertheless, the talents of Mrs. Gandhi could not remain hidden, and in spite of her devotion to the management of the house of her father, which was a great national service in itself, she continued to influence the Congress Party by her thinking and was the leader of what was known as "The Ginger Group", whose aim was to expedite measures to improve the lot of the teeming millions. Her devotion to truth and her fearlessness of purpose were proved when she differed from her father during her presidency of the Congress Party. This freedom of thought has been a special feature of the Nehru family. Mr. Nehru himself likewise publicly expressed his differences with his father in political matters during the latter's lifetime.

However, Mrs. Indira Gandhi's not being given any rank in the central cabinet during her father's prime ministership did silence some critical opponents of the Congress Party. But the nation as a whole had unstinted faith in Nehru's leadership and his integrity. This attitude of the masses was exhibited on the occasion of the election of the third Prime Minister of India when all the Chief Ministers of the various States of India unanimously resolved to elect Mrs. Indira Gandhi as Mr. Shastri's successor. The chief ministers are the leaders of their party in their states and are elected to the legislature by direct vote in the general elections. Hence they were expressing the opinion of the overwhelming majority of the masses of India. In spite of this, when a group of the members of the Parliament whispered that unanimity might look like the imposition of Mrs. Gandhi as the leader of a democratic party, the Working Committee of the Congress Party gave assent to the holding of the election by secret ballot. The voters were the Congress members of both the houses of the Parliament and the venue was the Central Hall of the Parliament House in New Delhi. When the results were announced Mrs. Gandhi received 355 votes while her rival Mr. Morarji Desai received 169. He was the first to congratulate Mrs. Gandhi soon after the election and later made public statements that he would always support Mrs. Gandhi's government as a true member of the Congress Party. He still holds a very high position in the Congress Party and is the head of a very important committee appointed by the Prime Minister. The activities of the Congress Party and the public reaction to the two catastrophes of the deaths of Mr. Nehru and Mr. Shastri within eighteen months have proved beyond all doubt that India has not only the greatest regard for the democratic way of life, but she applies it to her politics sincerely and enthusiastically. Let me quote an American journal: " (India) had proved for the second time in less than two years that it could lose a leader and not lose its head. That fact alone was encouraging to the free world. For all its problems, India has somehow managed to maintain a true working democracy. As such, it stands as a remarkable example in the eyes of the world as a clear alternative in Asia to Red China's Communism".

This dispassionate opinion is not a tribute but merely an expression of the facts and the history which the democracy of India is making. It is unfortunate that in the face of the ideological war between totalitarianism and the democratic way of life, and in the face of the fact that Communism carries on this struggle with a missionary zeal, the democracies in the free world are neglecting their duty towards the missionary aspect of the conflict by over-emphasizing freedom of thought and also by losing sight of the underlying unity of "Liberty, Equality and Fraternity" in the diversity of thought, feeling and actions which every democracy recognises and cherishes. That is, whereas equality and liberty are emphasized by the democracies, "fraternity" is neglected to the detriment of the cause of "equality and liberty". It is high time for the democracies of the world to realize this mistake, which is most prejudicial to the democratic way of life on our planet. It is worth noting that the USSR and Red China, in spite of their rift, seldom point out in public any weaknessess in the communistic way of life in their respective societies. Whether the curtain be iron or bamboo, the spirit of fraternity behind the scenes binds them because the purpose of communism is to win the ideological war, although it may, to be sure, be a kind of forced fraternity, an artificial brotherhood. But on the contrary, I find that whenever, a new steel plant is started in India or a new irrigation project is begun to mark the material progress of Indian democracy little or no publicity is given to such laudable achievements in the Western press and particularly in the countries that are aligned militarily, simply because India is a non-aligned country. On the other hand, most minor, sensational and misconstrued notions about India are given wide publicity in such countries. This is most unfortunate and is bound to mar the causes of freedom and democracy in the long run. We should not forget that in the complex international political situation of our times a non-aligned friend is better than an aligned enemy. The significance of this remark will become evident when I attempt to clarify some misunderstandings about the nonalignment policy of India in the next chapter.

It will suffice here to say that the election of the new Prime Minister of India on January 19, 1966, was clear proof of the determination of the Indian nation to sustain her democracy and to foster the spirit of the freedom of thought and action, and at the same time to re-establish the healthy traditions of giving credit to the sterling qualities of character and leadership which Mrs. Indira Gandhi possesses. The election of a woman as the Prime Minister of the largest democracy of the world is a unique example of the fact that equal opportunities for holding the highest office in politics without any distinction of caste, creed or sex do exist in a democracy. It must be borne in mind that Mrs. Gandhi is at the helm of affairs in India simply by virtue of her capability, her humanitarianism and her extreme devotion to the cause of the material and economic development of the whole nation. In this purpose as well as in the purpose of fostering international understanding and good will she resembles her illustrious father. She has endeared herself to the masses of India in a very short time. When she addresses the eager common people, workers, peasants and farmers or even highly educated gatherings, she establishes the same rapport with the audiences as Mr. Nehru used to do. When she speaks, she does so from the depth of her personality and the honesty of her purpose is crystal clear in her language and expression. This judgement is based on personal experience. There is no doubt that tremendous tasks face her and India's future. But she is judged by her peers to be the fittest person to meet all the challenges to the young democracy. India has great hopes from her leadership and expects that she will be able to create a much better and more realistic image of India abroad than both of her illustrious predecessors whom she admires and whose policies she is successfully carrying out. She is doing so not blindly but conscientiously and intelligently. She has independent judgement and originality, and I feel that if she is given fair chance by the leaders of the world she will very soon prove to be a unique international figure on account of her zeal for the maintainance of world peace in the interest of all of humanity.

CHAPTER XI

India's Policy of Non-Alignment

The foreign policy of most countries is intimately associated with their political, economic and cultural history. Whether statesmen establish friendly relations with other nations or injure the feelings of others depends on their political motives, economic urgencies and cultural background. This statement is probably more true today than it was ever before. The world has become small, and political, economic and ideological changes in one part of the world immediately and intimately influence the other parts. Never in the history of the world was internationalism so prominent and unavoidable for the political, economic and cultural development of individual nations as it is today. India's foreign policy particularly indicates the influence of its history on her statesmen. We have already mentioned how India attained independence through non-violent methods and how her veteran leader Gandhi ultimately succeeded in the unique experiment of applying love to politics. I wish therefore to try to throw some light on Gandhian ethics before discussing how and why India remained a non-aligned nation since she attained independence. Before going any further, however, I must emphasize the fact that the non-alignment of India is not a negative or passive attitude, but a positive and dynamic policy with the potentiality of contributing towards the well-being of the Indian nation as well as of the world.

The life history of Mahatma Gandhi was an experiment with truth, and this experiment ultimately demonstrated the victory of truth over untruth, of love over violence. Gandhi had abiding faith in the power of non-violence, and his followers demonstrated the application of his ideology during the mass movement of satyagraha, or non-violent truthful protest, against the high-

140

handedness of the British government in India. It is now admitted by all that the bloodless revolution led by Mahatma Gandhi was a unique example for the world. Albert Einstein, the well-known scientist philosopher, called Mahatma Gandhi

> A leader of the people, unsupported by outward author-ity. . . a victorious fighter who has always scorned the use of force: a man of wisdom and humility armed with re-solve and inflexible consistency, who has devoted all his strength to the uplifting of his people and the betterment of their lot; a man who has confronted the brutality of Europe with the dignity of simple human beings and thus at all times risen superior. . . Generations to come will scarce believe that such a one as this ever in flesh and blood walked upon the earth.

Einstein's remarks are well justified. Such great men appear very rarely in the world. The life and work of Gandhi are a constant reminder to the world that non-violence, the creed of the brave and courageous, is a practical mode of life and not a mere theory or a dogma. Gandhi was pragmatic. He never hated anyone and lived up to his ideals under all circumstances. His firm faith in the power of love was due to his conviction that even the meanest of the human species is capable of cultivating virtue because man is es-sentially spiritual and divine. If this ideology is practically fol-lowed there is no reason why man should not be able to bring about lasting peace on this earth. According to Mahatma Gandhi, man-kind has got to get over violence through non-violence. Hatred can be overcome only by love. This concept of non-violence is very old so far as Indian philosophy is concerned. It is at least as old as the Vedas. The Jaina Tirthankara Mahavira and the Buddha both ad-vocated non-violence as the highest virtue. They were religious teachers and as such they did not apply this virtue in secular cir-cumstances. Mahatma Gandhi, on the other hand, was a man of the masses, interested in the social, economic, political and down-to-earth well-being of his people. His purpose was to bring down heaven on earth by spiritualizing secular life. Gandhi was no doubt the first in the modern world to apply the concept of non-violence to practical life and to give it the widest possible connotation by identifying it with truth or God. He was led to this conclusion not merely by deliberation but by following the path of non-violence and thus by gradually realizing its true significance through experience. According to him non-violence is the way of life which is the means as well as the end of spiritual realizaton. It is the means because it brings about universal love, compassion, fellow-feeling and a sense of justice. It is the end because absolute non-violence is the highest virtue, the attainment of which would convert a man to God. Though the word non-violence is negative it has a positive import.

Gandhi's non-violence implies a classless society and a world without economic, political or social disparities. If the law of love is applied to the life of individuals and of communities it would bring about lasting peace to humankind. Gandhi pleaded that the application of non-violence to society could lead to great results provided people did undergo the requisite sacrifice. He wrote:

> Modern science is replete with illustrations of the seem-ing impossible having become possible within living mem-ory. But victories of physical science would be nothing against the victory of the science of life, which is summed up in Love, which is the law of our Being. I know that it cannot be proved by argument. It shall be proved by per-sons living it in their lives in utter disregard of consequences to themselves. There is no real gain without sacrifice and since the law of love is the realest gain, sacrifice too must be the greatest required.[1]

According to Gandhi one resorts to violence because he has lost faith in the dignity of man and has transgressed the duty of respect for life. He says that as long as organized violence and the race for armaments persist in the world we cannot boast of humanism, whether that humanism is supposed to be based on democracy or on communism. The presence of violence is proof of the bank-ruptcy of reason, the transgression of humanitarianism and the predominance of animal instinct over the spiritual urges of man. There can be no hope of rescuing humanity from atomic suicide until world politicians recognize the supremacy of the law of love in their political dealings. The path of non-violence advocated by Gandhi rises above all artificial barriers of caste, creed, religion and nationality and yet holds to the dignity of man in all spheres of life.

With this background of the philosophy of the sage and philos-opher who has been recognized as the father of Indian nation the

---

[1]Quoted in I. C. Sharma, *Ethical Philosophies of India,* p. 250.

reader can judge how the non-alignment policy of India is a positive attitude rather than a passive neutralism. Nehru, the direct political successor of Gandhi, adhered to this policy because he had full faith in the force of love. Besides this ideological background it must be remembered that India is most anxious to preserve her hard-won freedom. After the painful experience of British imperialism, which suppressed the Indian nation and posed before the world as a teacher for Indian democracy, it was natural for India to be cautious of all foreign powers. Imperialism can assume various disguises and India for the first few years of her independence was legitimately afraid of binding herself to any foreign nation. The bitter memories of the past, though now practically forgotten, did influence the attitude of liberated India towards the West to some extent. It was psychologically no surprise for newly freed India to look at political alliances with the West with caution if not with suspicion. Time and again India opposed colonialism and imperialism in the meetings of the United Nations. The United States has always been regarded as a lover of freedom and the enemy of colonialism, but India had to be hesitant in relying on the bonafides of the U.S., at least in the beginning. Although India has never mistrusted the U.S., its insistence on having political and economic ties without any military treaties was perfectly justified, keeping in view the psychological factors mentioned above. There is little doubt that today the intentions of the U.S. in Asia are more clearly understood than they were in the beginning.

I have already stated that the main task before Indian democracy is the economic development of the country. Here India stands on a par with the infant U.S. The U.S. faced the same problem in the beginning. It is a truism that a new nation cannot make economic progress if it becomes involved in international disputes requiring a military build up and an armament race. This is the reason the U.S. remained aloof from European ("international") affairs; that is why President Washington urged the young nation against "entangling alliances", and the U.S. adopted the famous Monroe policy of non-committal for a long time. This policy enabled the U.S. to have a breathing time to march on towards prosperity and progress without being hampered by the political complexities of Europe. India's economy had been terribly damaged by the British imperialists and required a complete overhauling to enable the average man to reach a minimum confortable standard of living. This could not be achieved without accelerating the production of agricultural raw material and consumer goods. Thus the improvement of agriculture by the introduction of mechanized farming, new methods of cultivation and the huge irrigation projects were the most decisive factors in achieving the aim of self-sufficiency in food. Similarly the development of small and heavy industry was essential for providing work for millions of unemployed persons and to raise the standard of living. Since India lacked machinery and technology she had to depend on foreign countries for the import of machinery and technological guidance for economic development. Such help would have been welcomed by any technologically advanced country, irrespective of its political ideology. Hence the policy of non-alignment with regard to military pacts either with the Western bloc or with the Russian bloc is both idealistic and pragmatic.

Moreover, India's economy is a mixed economy, i.e., an amalgam of socialism and democracy. As such it would be unwise for India to side either with the capitalistic bloc or with the communistic bloc. Indian economists, particularly Gandhian economists, think that neither an unrestrained capitalism nor iron-curtained communism can solve the economic problem. Extreme individualism, capricious free enterprise and cutthroat competition can lead to greed, exploitation of labor and monopolization of business and industry by a few capitalists. Similarly complete nationalization of trade, commerce, industry and agricultural reduces the individual to a mere cog in the social machinery. The golden mean between the two is partial national control over heavy industry and free enterprise in commerce, industry and agriculture. Neither the communes, which dismember family life, nor feudalism, which makes the landlord exploit the tenant, can be accepted as the solution to the problem of landless tenants and rural unemployment. Gandhism is the golden mean between the two extremes of communism and individualism and India is the first huge experiment in Gandhism. As such India's policy of non-alignment is also in keeping with its economc philosophy and the economic structure adopted by it. The U.S. on the one hand and the U.S.S.R. on the other have if not admired then respected India's non-alignment from this point of view, and both have helped India in the execution of her national economic plans. In fact, India's non-alignment makes her more deserving of economic aid from the West than the aligned nations.

Yet India's bonafides as a non-aligned nation are sometimes questioned. The result is that both power blocs hold back on giving generous economic aid to India. The Western powers appear to think that India is pro-communistic and the Russian bloc holds India to be pro-Western. However, Red China's attack on India has at least proved that the doubts on the part of the Western bloc were unfounded. With regard to the doubts on the part of the Communist bloc, it is hard to say whether they have been dispelled or not. So far as Red China is concerned there is not only doubt but firm conviction in the mind of Mao that India is not only pro-Western but anti-communist. In 1962 huge demonstrations in Red China exhibited photos of the three big enemies of China. Enemy number one was Mr. Kennedy, enemy number two was Mr. Nehru, and enemy number three was Mr. Khrushchev. There is no doubt that India today is decidedly opposed to Chinese communist imperialism. But this does not mean that she has joined the Western bloc. India's policy of non-alignment still holds for the ideological and economic reasons mentioned above. Nevertheless, India is not gaining enough in spite of her goodwill, sincerity and straightforwardness. This situation is detrimental not only to India under the present threat of Red China, but also to the cause of democracy and freedom as a whole. This aspect of the ideological war between communism and capitalism, between totalitarianism and democracy, must be borne in mind. It is a happy sign that affluent Western nations, particularly the U.S., have now realized that India's non-alignment should be considered an asset rather than a liability in giving her economic aid.

From the political point of view as well, India's policy of non-alignment is both necessary and justified. India is undoubtedly a democracy, perhaps even an ideal democracy since it has extended the adult franchise without any conditions. Even in the most advanced democracies like the U.S. there are conditions on voting eligibility. In communist countries, however, elections are a mere farce. India has made an attempt to solve social, political and economic disparity through constitutional means. Her political structure has now been established and it makes a unique combination of capitalism and socialism, free enterprise and controlled industrial production. Moreover, India has a firm faith in the power of the United Nations. Her statesmen believe that the purpose of the United Nations can be best achieved by minimizing groupism and power blocs. India therefore does not wish to divorce ideals from practice. As a member of the United Nations India is striving to set an example as a promoter of peace by following the policy of non-alignment and by accepting the maxim of "peaceful co-existence". Nehru's doctrine of the Five Principles proposed for adoption by the nations of the world a policy of peaceful co-existence as the cornerstone of an international philosophy of universal brotherhood which must ultimately be accepted and adopted by the United Nations.

India has promptly acted as a mediator and the promotor of peace whenever she had been called upon to do so. She has been most active in the United Nations and has played an important role in the solution of various international problems. She contributed by sending her troops to Korea. Similarly Indian military forces in the Congo have served under the command of the United Nations. India is always prepared to sacrifice her national interests for international peace. Her non-alignment therefore is not passive neutralism, but a positive pacifism. It is not generated out of hatred either for the Communist or the Western bloc but from the love of humanity. India does not advocate non-alignment as an expedient policy, but as a purposeful, constructive and dynamic ideology. Its method is non-violence and its goal is universal peace. This aspect of Indian statesmanship should never be lost sight of. It is sometimes said that such an attitude is merely idealistic. But the very fact that both power blocs are coming to realize the importance of a nuclear test ban treaty indicates that the realistic element of this idealism is gradually being recognized. It should not be forgotten that India is temperamentally and culturally urged to adopt non-alignment and that her earnest desire to promote peace is entirely humanistic. She does not want to be a partner or an accomplice to either bloc in aggravating the tensions of the cold war.

Now that both major power blocs have signed the partial nuclear test ban treaty it is evident that co-existence is beginning to be understood as a necessity. This atmosphere indicates that India's policy of non-alignment does have justification which is worth being heeded. It does not mean that the signing of such a treaty abolishes all chances of war, or that it means real love and friendship between opposing power blocs. But it does indicate an atmosphere of cordiality and co-operation, which is the purpose of the policy of non-alignment. It is also recognized that the presence of non-aligned nations would be necessary as a moral force in times of tension between the two largest power blocs.

India has not only set an example by being non-aligned so far as military pacts are concerned, but she has provided genuine leadership among the other non-aligned countries of Asia. Many of these uncommitted nations are young democracies anxious to main- tain peace, but they have yet to develop economically and politi- cally. India is the largest democracy among the non-aligned nations and her success or failure would undoubtedly affect the success or failure of all these nations. Red China has always felt jealous of the leadership of India and has feared the spread of democracy in Asia. Red China's imperalistic designs are being hampered by the promotion of India's policy of non-alignment. She has attempted and can be expected to continue to attempt to grab the uncom- mitted nations with a view to turning the whole of Asia into a communist continent. One way to achieve this mission is to lower the prestige of India and to impress upon the smaller non-aligned countries of Asia the idea that India is betraying the neutral zone. This was certainly one purpose implicit in Red China's attack on India. But there is no doubt that freedom is dearer to India than her political leadership in Asia. India has no imperialistic designs. She has not spent her money in building nuclear arms, although she is capable of doing so at present. Red China, on the other hand, wants to dominate not only Asia but the whole world. Her ex- pansionist policy requires that she be the unrivalled leader of Asia. By attacking India and by forcing her to join the Western power bloc, Red China could achieve this mission of eliminating India from the non-aligned countries. Luckily the Western powers came to the rescue of India at the critical juncture without jeopardizing her non-aligned status. This act of aid at the most opportune time on the part of Britain and U.S. was both prudent and generous. The moral obligation of India towards these two great nations owing to the timely aid of arms has become a very important factor to be reckoned with in future relations between these countries.

But does this mean that India's policy of non-alignment should be abandoned? An affirmative answer to this question would not come from a friend but from a foe of India. Asking India to join any power bloc and thereby giving up her non-aligned status would mean demanding political murder of India and hence of democracy in Asia. This is basically what Red China desires. Never was the time so ripe and the need so great for reaffirming faith in non-alignment on the part of India than in the critical situation created by the Red Chinese attack. The apprehensions of those (Western) countries which doubted the practicability of non-alignment on the part of India have automatically vanished as a result of the aggression of Red China. Not only the Western democracies but communist countries like Yugoslavia condemned the Chinese aggression. The prestige of India has increased in the West as well as in Southeast Asia. Red China's imperialistic designs have been revealed and condemned by all the reasonable nations of the world. This historical and political background proves that India's policy of non-alignment is justified because it is honest and ethical.

If India were to give up her non-alignment policy at this juncture it would not only mean that India repudiated its faith in love and non-violence but it would also mean the victory of Red China. The purpose of Red China to degrade India and hence to degrade democracy in Asia would be fulfilled. Red China's invasion of India proved beyond all doubt that India's policy of non-alignment was never anti-Western or pro-communist. Although it proves that Red China has exploited the idealistic aspect of Indian foreign policy, yet repudiation of the positive policy of non-alignment in the presence of the cold war has no justification. If one particular nation disregards human values and considers war the only solution to world problems this does not mean that saner nations should lose their sense or their equilibrium.

I have already stated that the non-alignment policy of India is honest because it is not generated out of any selfish motive of exploiting other nations. It is based on the cultural background of the Indian nation. Although the economic development of India is one pragmatic reason for the adoption of this policy it is not the dominant reason. The desire for world peace, universal brotherhood and goodwill on the part of India is genuine. Indian philosophy and religion, its ethics and political institutions are all based on the principle of universal love and human brotherhood. An ancient Indian verse in Sanskrit sums up this deep-rooted love of India in the following manner:

> A mean fellow inquires, belongs this person
> To my own caste, creed or religion?

> Broadminded persons always embrace
> As sisters and brothers the whole human race.

The Vedas declare that all human beings should co-operate, speak the same language, have the same goodwill and enjoy life together. Almost all the Vedic hymns used for daily prayer invoke peace for the whole universe. The gist of the daily prayer is given in the following popular verse of Sanskrit:

> "Sarve Bhavantu Sukhinah
> Sarve Santu Niramayah
> Sarve Bhadrāni Paśyantu
> Ma Kushchit Dukhabhāga Bhavet."

That is, "May all be at ease; may all be sinless; may all experience happiness; may none experience suffering." India's love for universal peace and her policy of non-alignment are the outcome of her ancient culture and philosophy, which are ingrained in the nature of every true Indian. In fact the adherence of India to the democratic way of life is fundamentally based on Indian culture. Let us therefore turn to the ideological background of Indian democracy.

CHAPTER XII

The Ideological Background of Indian Democracy

We have seen how the adoption of democracy and its progress in India have given confidence to its people, and how in spite of the odds India has successfully resisted the menace which overtook China. In spite of social, political and economic handicaps India has not given up her democratic ideals and is marching forward on the path of freedom and prosperity. She has not been obsessed by any traditions and superstitions usually present in ancient cultures. Revolution and violent changes take place in a society which is static, tenacious and unprogressive. When a culture is stale, anthropomorphic and dogmatic, it either leads its adherents to indolent self-centeredness and self-delusion or brings about a violent reaction which overthrows that culture itself. But when a culture is dynamic, ever-evolving and pragmatic, it helps a society or nation to adjust itself to the changing environment. The true picture of Indian culture is not known to the vast majority of people in the West, and hence there are misgivings about the nature of Indian democracy. The very fact that Indian culture has survived the test of time and still provides the broad base of modern democracy is proof of its being dynamic and evolutionary.

It is a strange phenomenon that India's culture in spite of being ancient is ever new and growing. It has absorbed into itself various elements of diverse cultures, nationalities and languages. Its "unity in diversity" has always been responsible for its evolution and adjustability. This special feature of Indian culture has saved its adherents from breaking loose with the past and adopting the destructive ideology of Communism. On the other hand Chinese culture was static and dogmatic. Confucianism, which is much praised by some scholars, requires the Chinese people to submit to the feudal system, to the authority of the king and to fate in order to attain manhood at its best. Such a culture was bound to lead the Chinese either to self-delusion or to Communism, which though the reverse of Confucianism in its opposition to feudalism, is at the same time equally dogmatic in emphasizing the submission to the system and to the dictator instead of the king.

Indian culture is not only dynamic and evolutionary, but also deeply spiritual in nature. When I use the word spiritual here I do not mean something concerning departed souls or ancestor worship popular in China and Japan. By spiritual I mean that inner aspect of human personality which expresses itself in the creation and appreciation of art, poetry, music, drama, sculpture and even of mechanical and technological devices, and which is regarded as the indwelling spirit or the divine element in man and cosmos. Without the acknowledgement of this positive immanent reality of the spirit a culture is bound either to degenerate into nihilism and inactivism or to a soulless totalitarianism. Moreover the scientific and logical basis of this spirituality of Indian culture (a detailed discussion of which is out of place here) gives conviction and confidence to its adherents, and thus gives them a unique power to outlive the storm and stress of life. It does not ask a person to renounce the active life, as many Western scholars have wrongly supposed. It is on the contrary, a positive practical philosophy which brings about a synthesis of the religious and the secular, the spiritual and the mundane, and of intuition and reason. Indian spirituality is a mode of life rather than a speculation. It aims at the integrated development of the individual as well as that of the society. Communism sacrifices the individual for the society and individualism tends to neglect social values. But Indian spirituality, which has taken root in Indian society during the past five thousand or more years, reconciles freedom of the individual and the demands of society. I would like to refer briefly to this aspect of Indian culture and also to the degeneration which has entered into the traditional aspect of this culture. This account will help the reader understand the potentiality of Indian culture to stand against totalitarian tendencies.

The keynote of the ancient culture of India is the acceptance of the one spiritual reality, the sole cause of the universe and of the diverse pluralistic universe with its diversities of individuals. In other words both the fundamental unity and the spatio-temporal diversity of the universe are accepted in Indian culture. The Vedas, the oldest recorded literature, propound the oldest scientific theory of the universe and base the constitution of the individual and of the society on that concept. It is worth noting that this theory neither denies the pluralistic nature of the spatio-temporal universe, nor rejects the divine unitive nature of God. Neither does it lean towards anthropomorphism nor repudiate spiritual reality. The cosmological, astrophysical, sociological, psychological and ethical aspects of knowledge are amalgamated and made the basis of science and life and theory and practice with logical consistency.

I will first give a brief account of this scheme of life for the reader and then point out how the positive culture of India, as opposed to China's negative culture, has served as a safeguard against Communism in this country. The sages of India, while setting out the various theories of the evolution of the universe, have referred to one dynamic theory called Pancha Parvā Vishva Vidyā, or the five-membered theory of the universe. This five-member theory of the universe mentions the five divisions of the one branch of the universe which stems from that central reality called Prajapati, or creative generator. Prajapati is that element which resides in the center of everything and which being itself unborn is the cause of the birth of the multiple universe. It has been called the "truth of truth" and the "center of centers." Its primeval evolute is Svayambhu Prajapati, or the cosmic center. According to this old theory, the five members or entitles of one branch of the universe are (1) Earth (entity), or Prithvi, (2) Moon (entity) or Chandra, (3) Sun (entity), or Surya, (4) Galactic center, or Parmeshthi (entity) and (5) Cosmic center, or Svayambhu Prajapati (entity). It is further mentioned that the earth revolves around the sun, moon revolves around the earth, sun revolves around its galactic center, which is the center of gravitation for numberless solar systems, and the galactic center itself revolves around the cosmic center. The cosmic center is the first evolute of the center of centers (Prajapati or Brahman) which is invisible, all-pervasive infinite power. The constitution of man has therefore been based on the analogy of the universe. Man is an integrated whole of body, mind, intellect (reason) and soul. The body represents the earth element, the mind represents the moon element, the intellect represents the sun element, and the soul represents both the Prajapati or galactic center, and the Svayambhu Prajapati, the cosmic center. It is necessary here to explain the two aspects of the soul or Atman. The Atman actually consists of (1) Mahān Atman, or great self and (2) Avyaya Purusha, or the invisible spiritual self. The great self consists of those tendencies and traits in the personality of an individual which he or she inherits from predecessors and transmits further to successors. This aspect of the soul corresponds to what in analytical psychology may be called the impersonal unconscious. The second aspect of the soul, Avyaya Purusha, the invisible spiritual self, is that imperishable transcendental aspect of the individual which is the real central spiritual existence.

Thus man is an integrated whole or four aspects, viz: (1) body, or Sharira, (2) mind, or Manah, (3) intellect, or Buddhi, and (4) soul, or Atman. However one individual may differ from another in the predominance of one of these aspects over the other three. A person physically stronger than others may have the predominance of the earth element in him and his other aspects of personality may be weak. Such a person would be fit for adopting a profession in which physical strength is the prerequisite. Similarly a person whose mental power is more predominant than the other three elements would be suited for the professions where skilled labor, art, engineering, etc. are necessary. The person with a predominant intellect would be fit for the administrative profession. Lastly a person with the spiritually predominant nature would be best suited for the professions of teaching philosophy and the priesthood. In fact, this is how the caste system of India was generated. Its original basis was not birth, but the natural inclination and the profession adopted by individuals. The physically predominated persons formed the caste known as Shudras, or the labor class; the mentally predominant were called the skilled labor class, or Vaishyas. Similarly the intellectually predominant joined the profession of Kshatriya, or administrative class. The spiritually predominant persons adopted the profession of teachers and spiritual guides whose aim in life was to promote the well-being of all human beings irrespective of caste, creed and nationality.

Corresponding to these four aspects of human nature and society have been laid down the four values of life. These four values or ends of life, which are called Purusharthas, or the purposes of man, are as follows: (1) Artha, or wealth (economic value), (2) Kama, or love (emotional value), (3) Dharma, or duty (ethical value), and (4) Moksha, or spiritual liberation or God-realization (spiritual value.) The dynamism and activism of this philosophy of life is evident since it recognizes all the four values as equally important for the integrated development of the individual and of society. Wealth or economic value is essential for the development of the physical body or the material aspect of society. Love or satisfaction of desires is required for the normal development of mind or the artistic aspect of society. Duty or ethical value leads to the intellectual development of the individual and the administrative or governmental aspect of society. Finally, spiritual liberation or self-realization brings about the development of the spiritual aspect of the individual and of the society. The recognition of individual differences so far as the physical, mental and intellectual aspects are concerned presupposes the necessity of freedom—social, political and ethical. It prompts man to accept the realistic differences between individuals so far as physical, mental and intellectual capabilities are concerned. It therefore not only forbids but disproves any forced equality amongst men. Individuals are not homogeneous, and the levelling down of society by any totalitarian method would be falsifying facts and going against nature. On the other hand the underlying spirit which transcends the physical and social differences makes Indians conscious of "unity in diversity" and "harmony in discord". Thus Indian democracy, which avoids both the extremes of totalitarianism and extreme individualism, is in keeping with the tradition, the philosophy and culture of India. India has adopted Western democracy and has accepted industrialization as the means of the economic and political development of her people. But she is temperamentally disinclined to crush her ethical and spiritual values by adopting totalitarianism as China has done.

A glance at the cultural background of China will support the view that India's culture has played a very important role in saving India from going Red. China's culture can be summed up in the following three dominant currents: (1) Cunfucianism, (2) Taoism and (3) Buddhism. Confucianism, which is still held to be the basic and the purely nationalistic trend of Chinese culture, advocates the submission of the individual to the head of the state and to the dogmatic rituals of society without freedom of choice. It also propounds the view that the best man is one who voluntarily subordinates himself to heaven. Taoism lays emphasis on the last aspect of Confucianism and ultimately advocates a philosophy of inactivity and passivity. According to it one must follow the Tao, or the way, and must not resist even death. In the last analysis Taoism turns out to be a philosophy of life which urges individuals indifference to all activity and resort to silence, separateness and solitude. Tao, or the eternal law, is not a positive spiritual principle, but something which can be identified with vacuity and nothingness. The acceptance of Buddhism, whose ultimate goal, Nirvāna, is the merging of the individual into nothingness (Sunyatā), was most suited to the agnostic and nihilistic mind of Taoistic China. Buddhism does not hold a belief in God either as a creator or as a positive power. According to it the goal of life is the annihiliation of human personality and the attainment of nothingness or vacuity. It is for this reason that in spite of being born in India Buddhism died out from the land of spirituality and sages, who have again and again asserted the positive existence of the eternal spirit. The only religion acceptable to China was the nihilistic religion of Buddhism. As a consequence Communism, which is based upon the negativistic philosophy of Karl Marx, could become the political way of life acceptable to China. It is no wonder that Mao Tse-Tung advocates violence as the only way to convert the whole world to Communism. The cultural background of China helps to explain its adherence to communism and totalitarianism.

India's culture has sustained her throughout. She has been able to survive devastating foreign attacks, atrocities of fanatic kings, like Aurangzeb, and British imperialism without losing her spirit. The body of India has been conquered by foreign invaders many times and such conquest has brought about social, political and economic degeneration from time to time. But her spiritual background, in spite of being overlaid for a time by the ignorance of the masses who fell victim to superstition and blind faith, still stands as the redeeming feature of Indian culture. I must mention here the degeneration of the caste system, which was originally viable and free from any hereditary bias. During the middle ages when India lost her political freedom many salutary traditions were lost and rigidity set in the caste system. The greatest misuse of the caste system appeared in discrimination against the so-called lower caste, the members of which were engaged in duties like scavenging, butchering and shoemaking. Such persons were in the course of time considered "untouchables" and lived outside the boundaries of the towns and villages. This social degeneration was definitely man-made and embodied the very opposite of the essence of Indian culture and philosophy. Even in the nineteenth century the pinch of this degeneration was felt by Indian reformers and spiritual leaders.

Swami Dayananda, the great spiritual leader of the nineteenth century, raised his voice against the minunderstanding and misuse of the caste system and led a revolution against social discrimination. His leadership was recognized, and after his death the "Arya Samaj" movement gained ground. Millions of Arya Samajists brought about an awakening in the country and helped in removing the blight of untouchability. Hindu religion, the quintessence of which is the philosophy of the great Bhagavadgitā, is against the spirit of racial or professional discrimination. The religious reformers of the nineteenth century emphasized this aspect of Hinduism and spiritually prepared the masses to oppose untouchability. In the twentieth century, particularly in nineteen-thirties, Mahatma Gandhi resumed the reformist movement and urged the Hindu masses to give up the superstitious notion of untouchability. He observed a fast, declaring he would not take food unless and until the so-called untouchables were allowed to enter the temples. His fast had a magical effect, and the temples were thrown open to all untouchables who were now designated "Harijans", or men of God. The purpose of mentioning these facts is to emphasize the fact that the problem of untouchability has been tackled in India gradually, systematically and culturally. It was after the attainment of independence in 1947 that untouchability could be legally banned. It was the gradual preparation for this event and the cultural background of India which led to the peaceful solution of the social problem. Not a single instance of violent protest can be cited in India with reference to the entry of so-called untouchables either into the temples or educational institutions.

If this blight of untouchability had continued to exist in India she might easily have succumbed to Communism. The oppressed untouchables could easily be swayed by the promises of equality glibly given by Red propagandists. There are many misunderstandings among Westerners with regard to the evils of the caste system in India. Most people in the West are given to understand that the so-called lower castes cannot change their profession or occupation. The caste system is in fact no bar to any individual so far as the adoption of any profession or occupation is concerned. There is no doubt that most of the so-called untouchables were backward educationally and economically. But they were not the only class of backward Indians. The schedule of backward classes in India includes many castes, including some castes of Brahmins. Moreover it must be remembered that even economically, caste is no help or hindrance. Misinformed Westeners are under the impression that higher castes, say Brahmanas or Kstariyas, are all rich and the lower castes all poor. This is not the case. A person may become wealthy through any business or any profession even if he belongs to the so-called lowest class. On the other hand it is noteworthy that the economic condition of those Brahmins who have not changed their priestly profession is the poorest. As a matter of fact the caste system in India does not exist in the form which the Westerner imagines. There are millions of Vaishyas (the third caste, in order of merit) and pauper Brahmins. So-called untouchables are big businessmen, industrialists, engineers, administrators, members of legislatures and ministers of the state and central cabinets.

This picture of the caste system is certainly different from the one depicted in the journals in the Western world. But it is the true picture of India, which is heading towards social, political and economic progress because her culture is not static. She is not opposed to economic, political and social changes. She has no prejudice against the use of machinery and automobiles. It is not the case that Indians were heathens before the British occupied India and became enlightened by the magical touch of British imperialism. On the contrary, adjustability—social, political and economic—is the very essence of Indian culture and philosophy. If the presence of the Western powers had been the sole cause of political and economic advancement the British and other European colonies of South Africa should have been as progressive as India. To strip India of her cultural and political history, to disinherit her from her spiritual heritage and to regard her as the creation of British liberalism is to deny the individuality of Indian democracy.

Modern democracy is no doubt a Western concept and its practice as a system of government began, developed, and reached its climax in the West. It is also true that Indian leaders like Gandhi and Nehru were educated in the West and were inspired by Western history and politics. But the adoption of democracy and its success in India would not have been possible if India had no cultural traits suitable to democracy. Gandhi dedicated his life to the cause of the freedom of India not only because he was educated in England. On the contrary, his being truly Indian in essence helped him in recognizing and respecting the integrity and the dignity of Indian culture. Patriotism is not generated by imitating a foreign culture but by recognizing the worth of one's national heritage. I have already mentioned that many of the sons of the rulers of Indian states were educated in England. But none of them was inspired to turn into a patriot. On the contrary, they became the enemies of the freedom movement.

Even Nehru might not have became a national leader if he had not come in touch with Gandhi. The aim of his getting an education in England was to prepare him to become an administrative officer. Luckily he could not take the competitive examination for joining the Indian Civil Service because of the age limit. Had he joined the Indian Civil Service he would have retired as a deputy commissioner or as the judge of the Indian high court. No one would even have heard of Nehru in the Western world and the Indian nation would have been deprived of his services. Nehru's contact with Gandhi was a most important event in the political history of India. Gandhi, as I have already stated, was the embodiment of Indian culture. His concepts, methods and goals were purely Indian.

Before Gandhi the national movement was led by the great patriot, Lokmanya Balgangadhar Tilak. This great leader of India was not educated abroad. His greatest academic achievement is his immortal work, "Gita Rahsya", or the "Secret of the Philosophy of the Bhagavadgitā." He has called attention to the activism of this philosophy. He lead his life according to the precepts of the Gita, and even Gandhi followed him in this respect. Had Tilak not died suddenly Gandhi would have remained in the background. This dynamic person gave a powerful push to the freedom movement, and even after his death his views were the source of inspiration to all Indian patriots and political leaders. My purpose in referring to the deep-rooted love of Mr. B.G. Tilak for Indian culture is to point out how Indian philosophy and culture have played an indispensable role in the political history of India.

This aspect of the evolution of Indian democracy is little known and is therefore neglected. There is no doubt that economic and technological aid from the West has strengthened and will continue to strengthen Indian democracy. But the progress of democracy in India is inseparably associated with Indian culture. The leaders of India are conscious of this fact. The introduction of decentralization is the biggest achievement of the democratic experiment in India. I have already mentioned how freedom has reached every village in India by means of the establishment of the Panchayat (village assembly) system and how this system is helping the economic development of India. I have stated that India is rich in resources and that the economic development of the country will be expedited when all resources are exploited by the adoption of technology and automation. India can make rapid progress for two reasons. First, the venture of economic planning in India has been started in the atomic age. The existence of a highly developed technology will eliminate the trial and error learning of the Indian nation for adopting mechanized farming and producing synthetic materials. India has gained and will continue to gain from the experience of highly developed Western science, technology and industry. She has only to apply the experience of Western scientists and technologists to the unexplored and unexploited regions of her natural resources. That is why India is hopeful as are her economic and technological Western assistants. The United States in particular is now vigilant in seeing that economic aid to underdeveloped countries is fully utilized and therefore justified. Every U.S. ambassador and every economic adviser who visits India pleads the cause of economic aid to India. This is because these visitors personally observe democracy at work. India herself is confident that she will be able to pay off loans granted to her by the U.S. government for industrial development. Secondly, the average man in India is enthusiastic about the economic development of his country. This enthusiasm, as I have already stated, is due to the introduction of democratic decentralization which has given political and administrative responsibility to the average man. Thus the introduction of machines and democratic decentralization will doubtless accelerate the economic and the political development of Indian democracy.

I have also mentioned that the election of the village assemblies, which is now political, was virtually already existent in the past. Before political independence this elected body had limited powers and mainly acted as a social organization. However, its presence as a social structure helped Indian politicians to conceive its structure politically and thus utilize a cultural tradition for political development. Incidentally, the introduction of political election in the village assemblies and in the state assemblies has had its own influence in breaking social barriers as well. Previously, a self-conceited and orthodox Brahmin might not have wished to visit the house of a so-called untouchable. But today when such a Brahmin stands as candidate for election to the village assembly he depends on the vote of the previously unwelcome untouchable. He not only condescends to enter the home of the so-called low caste person but humbly requests his vote. He even invites the so-called untouchable to his own house and dines with him. Thus the introduction of democracy in India has been influenced by its culture and has in turn influenced Indian culture for the better.

Hindu religion has no prejudice against sex and birth control. India has no national pride or false political notions that may stand in the way of her family planning program which has now been launched seriously by the Indian government. For some time there was some apprehension among Indian leaders that the introduction of family planning might lead to religious objections on the part of the illiterate masses of India. But after the family planning program was introduced and the advantages of a planned family were known to the people of India, the illiterates came forward to adopt the methods of birth control. The liberalism of Indian culture is a unique factor. I was surprised to know that in some states in the Western world a doctor is not allowed by law to advise on family planning. In India family planning is not only a very important function of the medical department of all the governments but it is becoming a vogue. I wonder on what grounds the Indian masses can be considered backward when they are not obsessed or repelled by such ventures and when they gladly co-operate in birth control.

In Red China family planning was introduced for some time to solve the food problem. It is said that during this campaign the whole of China was ringing with birth control propaganda. All government officials and the members of the Communist party were engaged in pushing the campaign to succeed. But when the Communist dictator of China was given to understand that the adoption of family planning might lead the world to suspect that Communism was unable to solve the problem of population, the whole process was reversed. Counter-propaganda was begun and family planning was condemned outright. The imperialistic pride of China, her preference for manpower at the cost of quality, and Chairman Mao's attempt to prove that Communism is a panacea are hindrances in the solution of China's problem. If Communism gives promise of solving the problem of population China will continue to worship the ideology. But India has no such pride and prejudice. She is prepared to accept family planning, and therefore her population problem does not need any false ideology to control it.

India's cultural background makes her people adjust easily to new situations. For example, emancipation of women, which started in Europe in the nineteenth century, has given equal right to women in society and politics in most of the countries of Europe and in practically the whole of the West. In India this movement has taken long strides, and Indian women today occupy a most important place in national and international politics. This is all due to the cultural background of India. According to Hindu culture woman is the object of respect. A Sanskrit verse says that wherever women are worshipped, there the gods move about. Hindu religion believes both in an infinite impersonal and personal God who manifests himself in every critical age to restore virtue and piety. Whenever the personal God or the incarnation of God is worshipped, he is never worshipped alone but in a pair. God is said to be Ardhanarishwar, i.e., half-woman. When Krishna, the propounder of the well-known philosophy of the Bhagavadgitā, is worshipped, he is worshipped along with his consort, Radha. When the devotees utter his name, they first utter the name of his consort and repeat "Radha Krishana" again and again. Similarly when the name of Rama, another incarnation of God, is uttered, it is prefixed by the name of his wife, Sita. Even in the hoary past women in India had a unique status. No religious ceremony performed by a man was considered complete without the participation of his wife. As early as 1000 B.C. there were women philosophers and teachers. There is ample evidence for the presence of co-education in the hermitages during that period. Kalidasa, the greatest poet and dramatist of Sanskrit (1st century B.C.), who is known as the "Shakespeare of India", and whose immortal play "Shakuntala" has been translated into almost all the languages of the world, was educated by his wife, Vidyotma. Women had greater freedom than men. The ceremony of Svayamvara, in which the woman was allowed to choose her own husband, was very common. Although these cultural traits centering on the equality of women were suppressed during the subjugation of India to the Muslims and later on to the British, yet they were dormant in Indian society. During the struggle for independence Indian women stood shoulder to shoulder with men and made great sacrifices. Millions of women had come forward actively to offer satyagraha and to court imprisonment. Mrs. Kamala Nehru was one such woman. Her death was itself a sacrifice to enable Mr. Nehru to serve his country. Similarly the names of Kasturba Gandhi, Mrs. Vijya Laxmi Pandit, Mrs. Sarojini Naidu, Rajkumari Amrita Kaur, Mrs. Indira Gandhi and others will ever shine in the political history of India, reminding us of the greatness of Indian women. During an armed revolt in India against the British more than hundred years ago, a brave woman, Laxmi Bai, the queen of Jhansi, a great heroine, led this war of independence. She fought on the battlefield and was killed in action. She fought using a sword in each hand simultaneously. Her name is the source of great inspiration to women in India even today. In brief we can say that in every generation India has produced millions of women whose existence helped to civilize the country. Their warmth of heart, self-sacrificing zeal, unassuming loyalty and strength in suffering when subjugated to trials of extreme severity are among the glories of this ancient race. The position of Indian women is most important and exalted not only in the home but in politics. Today about ten percent of the members of the Indian parliament are women. Similarly hundreds of Indian women are elected members of the state legislative assemblies. In every state there are women cabinet members. There are women ministers in the Federal cabinet, women governors, ambassadors and administrators in India. It is noteworthy that India is the country which has provided the first woman president of the United Nations. Although India is a young democracy it has excelled even the oldest democracies in granting opportunity to women in politics. These are the various cultural factors which have helped the adoption and the progress of democracy in India.

India's special problems and her own cultural background make Indian democracy a unique system of government. Democracy is bound to differ in its operation from country to country and from culture to culture. Indian democracy is an amalgam of Eastern and Western cultures. India has accepted the democratic constitution, free enterprise in trade and commerce, and the acceleration of industry. But she has not and will not give up her spiritual values. Man is superior to the animals not only because he has superior knowledge but also because he cherishes values. Values always make man human. But we must always remember that man, the maker of science and systems, is himself above ideologies. We shall conclude our book with this theme.

CHAPTER XIII

Conclusion:
Man is Higher than Ideologies

In the preceding chapter I have attempted to give an account of India's efforts to make social, political and economic progress. In spite of her handicaps she has been striving to solve these large problems and has at the same time been trying to remain non-aligned. Her cultural background and her economic problems, combined with the peculiar political environment of the contemporary world, justify her remaining noncommitted in the cold war. My observations about Pakistan and the conclusions drawn from the actual events in Asia can be verified by the reader. One late development between Pakistan and Red China is Pakistan's concluding an agreement with China to open an air route between these two countries (1964). Pakistan is the first non-Communist country to enter into such an agreement. Pakistan concluded this transaction in spite of the protest of the United States. This fact underscores my observation that Pakistan's self-interest supercedes her internal and her foreign policy, and that the West must be cautious and vigilant in dealing with this fanatical country. While most Western powers have signed the partial nuclear test ban treaty with Russia, and while China is the only country in the world today to condemn such attempts at minimizing the nuclear race, Pakistan is flirting with China. The only common bond between Pakistan and Red China is their hatred towards India. Pakistan hopes to gain materially from Red China, because the latter is the deadly enemy of India. Perhaps the leaders of Pakistan forget that in spite of the treaty of co-existence between India and China, and in spite of India's constant support of China's admission to the United Nations the reward of India's unselfishness was Red Chinese aggression. It is really strange that Red China, which dares even to threaten Russia, her life-giver, should be expected to nourish Pakistan, the baby whose protection is bound up with SEATO and CENTO. This is one more consistent inconsistency of Communist China. The Western nations, and in particular the United States, are well-advised to judge India's foreign policy with reference to these events. Not only is non-alignment the best policy for India and for Asia today, but any other policy would be detrimental to the interests of the Western powers themselves. One thing is quite sure: the opposition of Pakistan to India's joining the Western bloc. If by any chance India were to show even the slightest indication of joining the Western bloc, Pakistan may change positions suddenly. The sole purpose of Pakistan is to blackmail India's catastrophic plight. Even then, India can, under no circumstances, afford to see Pakistan go down. She has never resorted to any propaganda against Pakistan. It is necessary for the democracies to understand the intentions of India and to genuinely appreciate her policy of non-alignment.

At the same time India also needs to understand the attitude of the Western bloc. At its birth India was skeptical about the intentions of the U.S.A. in Asia. India had not forgotten British imperialism and was undoubtedly suspicious of all countries. She shunned all strings and conditions attached to economic aid. Consequently she suffered and could not get as much financial help as was necessary for her speedy development. The U.S.A.'s policy towards colonialism in Asia was also not well-defined in the beginning and her part in the war in Vietnam has not exactly helped to make matters any more clear. Hence misunderstandings were bound to arise on both sides. Pakistan's malicious propaganda, without India's counter-propaganda, has fanned misunderstandings about India in the West. I strongly feel that India has committed a blunder in tolerating the false propaganda of Pakistan in the West. It was essential to clarify the issues to the West. The people of the U.S.A. are receptive and open-minded. They are amenable to reason and to facts. But when facts are not forthcoming, the only way open to a person is to decide *ex parte,* or else make no judgment at all, of course. During one year's stay in the U.S.A. (1962-63), and again in 1965 and 1966 I addressed scores of gatherings and satisfied their curiosity about the issues between India and Pakistan. When the American people come to know the facts in the case, they are simply surprised and at once feel sympathetic towards India. The people of the United States have no ill-will against India. I am writing these facts not out of any personal prejudice, but as a matter of simple witness. It is essential for India to understand the U.S.A. better and to shake off all false notions, prejudices and preoccupations.

Misunderstandings arise because of ignorance of facts, and interest in knowing the facts is blunted due to misunderstandings. Thus a vicious circle is started which blurs our whole view and blinds the politicians as well as the people. There are numberless misunderstandings about the U.S.A. in India which must be removed by the honest efforts of the intelligensia of India and of the U.S.A. Millions of Indians do not know what capitalism is at work. They are under the false impression that Americans are indolent and ease-loving, and that they are rolling in dollars, drinking champagne and dancing round the clock, while millions in the world cannot enjoy two square meals a day.

Such a distorted and purely prejudicial view about the American people must be corrected before anything can be done to bring about understanding between East and West. Only when a person visits the U.S.A. and observes how hardworking and diligent the people of this country are can he realize how vitiated his opinion was about American life and the American people. I have already stated that capitalism is successful in the U.S.A. because the employer and the employee, the capitalist and the laborer, the technologist and the unskilled worker, the scientist and the schoolmaster, in short, every able-bodied, sensible and reasonable person in the U.S.A. works diligently at his job. I wonder why foreign observers in the U.S.A. neglect this dynamic aspect of American life. If the U.S.A. is the richest country in the world today, is it because she had any empire, or because she exploited any other nation of the world? On the contrary, nations like Britain and France, which had huge empires and which did get material benefits at the cost of their subject countries, were not imitated by the U.S.A. I can understand the jealousy of other nations toward the United States. But this jealousy is quite unjustified when we face the fact that the sole cause of the prosperity of U.S.A. is the honest labor, the constant effort to develop education, industry, agriculture, science and technology. We should not forget that the early settlers came to the continent of America without any wealth. They were displaced persons. But they were determined to build their future and they succeeded in their mission. The people of the U.S.A. have set a unique example for all countries and this example ought to be emulated. The people of the United States have no time to think of establishing any empire because they are almost entirely devoted to the development of their own country, the exploitation of the natural resources of their own land.

The argument that the U.S.A. needs markets outside and hence political influence in the world is no argument to prove that it wants to build any empire. First, it may be pointed out that the foreign trade policy of the U.S.A. is most liberal. She imports manufactured goods from almost all the countries of the world. Not only this, but a huge amount of her treasure goes to foreign aid for the welfare of underdeveloped countries. Not only the democracies but even Communist countries are benefitted by the foreign aid programs of the U.S.A.! The tragedy is that most of the countries which receive the aid not only often misuse it, but instead of being grateful they sometimes seem to blame the U.S.A. The humanistic and selfless urge of the U.S.A. to help other countries is evident from the fact that in spite of reaping a harvest of criticism instead of appreciation, she is continuing to aid underdeveloped nations. I do not understand in what sense the U.S.A. is inferior to any other nation of the world. She not only cooperates with the Eastern as well as the Western countries to preserve peace, to eliminate want and hunger and to foster science and technology, but she also spends more money than all other nations in such projects. Why should all these facts be overlooked? Why is this humanistic aspect of the people of the U.S.A. not regarded as their greatest contribution to fostering goodwill and international understanding? There is no doubt that U.S. foreign policy in general, and economic aid in particular go to prove that man is higher than ideologies.

Another important fact that I would like to emphasize here is that the United States and her people have to undergo considerable turmoil for all these humanistic and altruistic activities. As I have already stated, the average man in the U.S.A. has to pay the heaviest taxes in the world, perhaps with the exception of the average Englishman. The people of the U.S.A. have to work harder and exert themselves more than the people of other countries of the world for leading a normal life with modern amenities. The prosperity of the United States is hard-earned and based on inspiration as well as perspiration, the urge for work as well as actual diligence. Hence the progress of this nation should not arouse jealousy or criticism among other nations, particularly among the democratic nations. As a matter of fact, Russia, the greatest Communist country, is trying to follow the footsteps of the U.S.A. in making all its efforts to increase production, to build up the economy by fostering industry, and by resorting to scientific and technological research for this purpose. If we were to compare the American economy with the Russian economy, the main difference between the two would be that whereas the U.S.A. has followed the path of freedom and the spontaneous urge to develop, the U.S.S.R. is imposing labor on her people. Whereas the U.S. economy is a natural growth, the Russian economy is a mechanical build-up. The former is free, purposive and teleological, directed towards the development of the individual's personality, the latter aims at the blind identification of the individual with a mechanical political structure. The former is humanistic and the latter is mechanistic.

In adopting the teleological rather than the mechanical path of progress, India will find it necessary to have a thorough knowledge of the nature and function of the American system. There is no doubt that the leaders of India have asserted again and again that the goal of Indian democracy is based on the liberty, equality and the dignity of the individual, and in this respect it is on a par with American democracy. Referring to this urge of India, Nehru, while addressing the American people in his television address from Washington, D.C. on the 18th of December, 1956, said, "Five years ago, a professor of an American university visited me in Delhi, and gave me a gift which I have treasured greatly. That was a mold in brass of Abraham Lincoln's right hand. It is a beautiful hand, strong and firm and yet gentle. It has been kept ever since on my table, and I look at it every day and it gives me strength." This perhaps may give you some idea of our thinking and our urges in India. For above all, we believe in the liberty, equality, the dignity of the individual and the freedom of the human spirit. This spontaneous expression of Nehru speaks for itself. But all our leaders do not have the same insight and sincerity of purpose as Nehru had. The result is that even his most trusted diplomats undo what Nehru has done when they misunderstand and misrepresent the

U.S.A. and create ill-will for India in the Western hemisphere because of misconceptions about the U.S.A. One particular diplomat of India has done great harm to the cause of India in the U.S.A. and has created unnecessary and unjustified rancor toward India by his cynical and conceited way of behaving in press conferences and public appearances in the U.S.A. I was stunned to hear from many cultured men of the U.S.A. that such a responsible person should behave in such an irresponsible manner in public and should give an impression which is entirely contrary to India's culture, politeness and love of man. To behave cynically with people who are earnestly eager to know how Indian democracy is progressing is not only unwise, but immoral and contrary to the decency and hospitality for which India is so famous. It was a revelation to me when I visited the U.S.A. and when everywhere I heard a unanimous version of the awkwardness and the cynical and sinister attitude practised upon the people of the U.S.A. by that particular diplomat. Whatever might have been the reason for such awkward behavior, it has done great harm to the prestige and goodwill of India in the U.S.A. not only among statesmen and politicians, but also among the educated and cultured citizens of America. I strongly feel that the politicians of India ought to visit the U.S.A. not as official appointees, but as informal visitors and get an orientation before occupying any responsible political or administrative position. The mutual understanding of the U.S.A. and India is of vital importance not only for these two countries but for the preservation and fostering of democracy in Asia as well as in the West.

The people of the U.S.A. are eager to learn and concerned about the progress of India. When I found that mere lack of facts about Kashmir had been responsible for wrong impressions about the intentions of India towards Pakistan, I related facts. On hearing what I said, and on satisfying their curiosity about certain problems, I found that every one was not only convinced but expressed his or her sympathy and love for India. The American people are humane, sympathetic, and most affectionate. I had no previous acquaintance or correspondence with Americans. I visited the U.S.A. as a teacher and delivered speeches without any previous preparation, giving actual facts and answering questions of my audiences. I found them cordial, accommodating and most cooperative.

Man is undoubtedly higher than ideologies and human problems are more urgent than any social, political and even moral disciplines, which are all man-made. No ideology however promising and convincing can ever be accepted by people if it cannot solve their burning problems. Similarly no ideologist can be held high by the citizens of a nation if he does not "deliver the goods" which his ideology promises to yield. I have spoken about the promises of democracy and also the achievements of democracy in India. I have referred to the services and sacrifices of Gandhi and Nehru as the unique leaders of the Indian nation, and I have pointed out that the picture of India's future is not gloomy. There is no doubt that so far India has resisted the Red menace and has stuck to its culture and democratic ideals. But this does not mean that all is well with India, Indian politics and the Indian people. There are great dangers lurking in the path of Indian democracy. I cannot conclude this chapter without referring to the pitfalls and stumbling blocks in the way of India's progress. Unless our leaders are cautious and conscientious about attacking these drawbacks and defects, India is bound to be enveloped and engulfed by the Red fire which is spreading rapidly and perceptibly in Asia. Let this be my note of warning to my own countrymen and a signal against overoptimism in national and international politics.

These lurking dangers are social, political, and cultural. Let me dilate upon these, though briefly, to give both the sides of the picture of India. I will first refer to the social dangers to democracy in India. The reader might be surprised that after depicting the advantageous aspects of the social traditions of India I am now going to contradict my view by saying that there are social obstacles in the way of Indian democracy. But when I refer to the details of the misuse of the social structure of India on the part of the politicians, it will become evident that the fault lies with the personal motives of those who want to attain power by hook or crook. In order to clarify this point I shall have to explain once again what is the real nature of the caste system in India today.

There are a number of misunderstandings about the working of the caste system in India. There is no doubt that in the past it was based on the aptitude and the profession adopted by a person or a group of persons. It was both a division of labor and a social classification with the possibility of moving from one caste to the other. Intercaste marriages and change of caste itself were permitted. But as time passed the spirit of the system was neglected and many injurious conventions set in. In due course the caste system became very complicated and thousands of castes and sub-castes came into existence. These castes within castes had no religious or moral sanction but were accidental growths, resulting in tight compartmentalism only from the point of view of inter-dining and intermarriage. To a Westerner, the caste system even today means an economic classification, and hence he thinks that India's economic progress is necessarily hampered by the caste system. But this is actually not the case. I have already pointed out that the professional and economic structure of the caste system does not exist today as it did long ago. The caste today means a social group whose members may belong to any of the four kinds of professions. This group tends to remain narrow in the matters of inter-marriages, co-dining, etc. This groupism is also now on its way to breaking down. But a vast majority of Indians are very tenacious about it. This tenacity again is not due to any economic reasons or even to intellectual pride. It is not that, say, the Brahmanas, or Kshatriyas, who in the past were proud of their being associated with higher duties, refuse to have their children married in the other castes, but even the member of the so-called "backward" class, say, the barber caste (which was supposed to be a labor caste and hence a lower class) would not tolerate his son or daughter getting married in the Brahmana or Kshatriya caste! A false sense of superiority of one's own group has brought about these artificial walls between various groups. This groupism is purely accidental and its rigidity differs from state to state and even from city to city in India. In some areas it is most rigid, and the so-called different castes (which actually means groups or social communities, as I have explained) have different cremation grounds.

This is, however, absolutely against the spirit and even the scripture of Hinduism. There are some such communal groups which are most fanatic not only about intermarriage, but in all social, political and administrative dealings. This fanaticism is most dangerous because it sometimes leads to great injustice and nepotism. I would not blame the average man in this connection. The majority of people are illiterates who although orthodox in their social views are not tenacious. If they are properly treated by the educated, and if the misuse of groupism is brought home to them, they respond positively and are prepared to shed useless social customs. But the trouble is that the political climbers and the election seekers exploit orthdoxy and false social traditions. The political parties, whether traditional, progressive or Communist, foster social groupism and nominate their candidates for election from various constituencies on this basis. This jeopardizes the national interest, although a particular party or a group of that party may win elections. This precarious situation was the cause of the crushing defeat of the Congress Party in some constituencies during the general elections of 1962. Even the election of the Communist party members in Kerala in 1957 was the result of this exploitation of social and communal feelings. Communism can put on any garb and sneak into power. The top ranking leaders have not seriously tried to remove this evil. Even most highly educated politicians of India practice nepotism and favoritism. When a highly placed politician or administrator fills governmental vacancies by recruiting his kith and kin, neglecting the merits of the other candidates, the rejected and highly-qualified intelligent young people are bound to be frustrated. Nepotism is undoubtedly one of the gravest dangers to Indian democracy. It has entered the portals of universities as well and thus the frustration among the intellectuals is increasing day by day. I will refer to this danger shortly again. But I would like to add here that the interests of democracy are at stake as long as nepotism reigns supreme in the academic field. There are a few groups among the business community in industry, trade, and commerce which are notorious for this kind of nepotism. These conditions are most frustrating and call for an immediate and strong remedy.

I have already stated that political interests lead to the misuse of social traditions. In fact most of the dangers to Indian democracy are due to the strong desires of some people to capture political power at any cost. A political party which wants to win elections uses all sorts of tactics to woo the electorate. A party which is sure to win elections due to its prestige or influence sometimes nominates those candidates who can pay hundreds of thousands of rupees to the party concerned. In many states the parliamentary nominations in such political parties are almost sold at auction! This is a most unsavory part of Indian politics. If democracy degenerates into bargain, and if parliamentary membership can be bought only by the millionaires and multi-millionaires, then the future of India is dim indeed. This practice is not universal, but it is no doubt there. The result is that many intellectually superior and highly educated persons who can purge Indian politics of its impurities are debarred from fighting elections. It is a pity that Mr. Nehru was not able to remedy this cancerous growth in Indian politics. So far as I can see this disease is aggravating day by day, and the intellectuals shun politics and regard it a dirty game. If all capable persons cut themselves off from politics and the evils are allowed to grow, mal-administration, inefficiency and corruption are bound to bring about the collapse of Indian democracy.

Among the cultural dangers to democracy in India are linguism and regionalism. The language problem, however, is not as serious as Western people take it to be. There are a few fanatics who either overemphasize the spread of Hindi, the national language of India, or oppose it tooth and nail. It is an admitted fact that one of the indigenous languages must be the national language of India. Hardly two per cent of the Indians speak or write English correctly. Since Hindi is the language understood and spoken by a large majority of people in India, it was constitutionally adopted as the national language. Non-Hindi speaking states will take some time to develop this language. But the picture is not gloomy. If these states could pick up the English language so well that some of their inhabitants excelled even Englishmen in writing, there is no reason that they will not excel the writers from Hindi-speaking provinces when they come to learn it well. Linguism as a problem is bound to vanish in due course.

Regionalism exists in some states. But the Indian constitution is the greatest safeguard against this danger. In some newly-formed states, however, there is a peculiar kind of regionalism. Influential persons may capture political power in a given state and then recruit administrators and officers from their own particular area or territory. When such nepotism is resorted to in the academic field, it is disastrous. When an inefficient, arrogant and nepotistic person becomes president of an academic institution, he will almost certainly bring about the ruin of education and also foster frustration among the intellectuals. One university in India had the ill-luck of being put under the control of such a narrowminded, prejudiced and intriguing president whose appointment was supported by the politicians who mattered. He ruled the university supremely, without bothering about rules and regulations, harassing all personnel from top to bottom, insulting the professors of national and international repute, and manipulating almost all appointments to suit his own whim and intriguing nature. He had been brought up in an atmosphere of intrigue in the princely states, and he began to play one teacher against the other, creating a system of espionage among the members of the teaching staff as well as among students, holding a sort of a court of his informants at his residence frequently. Many capable and outspoken professors became sick and tired of his dirty politics and dissociated themselves from the university. Many intelligent and efficient teachers who refused to be his informants and flatterers were obliged to quit. They secured positions in other universities thereby depriving that university of their talents and efficiency. Some professors could not leave the university for personal reasons and had to endure insults frequently inflicted upon them by the dictator-president. But they resented his high-handedness, talked about his unjust decisions, hated his arrogance and groaned under his tyrannous rule. Not a word was uttered against him in his presence and not a line of protest against his overlordship and espionage was published in any paper. His close associations with top-ranking politicians both in the state and in the federal government scared the staff. Nepotism still triumps over democracy in India. Professional teachers' unions, as in the developed countries, might be a partial answer to the problems here presented.

I have stated plain and simple facts and depicted a true picture of a real situation. The reader can judge for himself what frustration the intellectuals must have experienced in such a suffocating atmosphere, and how much they must have been disgusted with democratic rule in India when, in spite of all this, that same president was given an extension to continue in his position after the expiration of his term of office. Whereas in a democracy like the United States freedom of speech permits even a government employee to express his personal opinion and even his criticism of government policy, in India it is often not possible for a government servant even to state facts without fear of losing his or her job. This suppression of government employees is a relic of British imperialism, and it is very strange that Indian democrats have not criticized or attacked this tradition in the interest of efficiency and fair play. Unless this timidity is overcome political freedom in India will never be followed by intellectual freedom, which is a prerequisite to the preservation of political freedom and the solidarity of the Indian democracy.

To sum up, the dangers lurking in Indian democracy are potentially disastrous and ought to be removed or at least minimized as soon as possible. Nepotism and the suppression of the intellectuals are the gravest of all dangers. If democracy vouchsafes equal opportunity to all individuals irrespective of caste, creed, sex and locality, the political climbers and the dictators in government and the universities ought to be brought to book, and government employees, particularly intellectuals, ought to be allowed to speak the truth in the interest of the masses. The future of India in general and of Indian democracy in particular depends not upon the columns and figures of the five-year plans, but upon the human material, especially upon the intelligent human material of India. Nothing is dearer to an intellectual than his love of truth and his integrity. It is highly fitting that Indian democracy above all should vouchsafe real freedom to, and uphold the dignity of man, failing which chaos and confusion, blackmailing and blasphemy, and corruption and callousness, which are the signs of Red fever, are bound to prevail. However, I am confident that India will not show a bankruptcy of intelligence, and that good sense will ultimately prevail on her political scene. The sooner it happens, the better it will be for the overall development of Indian democracy.

I have stated as frankly as possible the various factors which have strengthened or weakened Indian democracy. Democracy's success is the success of freedom and the dignity of man. Man is higher than ideologies, because it is man who conceives an ideology and not the ideology which conceives man. India has always regarded man as the highest reality, even though due to political vicissitudes human values have been eclipsed in this country too frequently. Reassertion of economic, social, political and spiritual values is the crying need, not only in India, but in the whole world today. Democracies and Communistic countries as well claim to aim at the well-being of man and international peace. The goal can be achieved if we recognize the importance of human values. Man is man, whether he lives in the Orient or in the Occident. His needs and urges, his appetites and desires and his joys and sorrow are always the same. Once this aspect of human nature is realized, ideological and cultural differences automatically vanish. The hackneyed lines, "East is East and West is West and never the twain shall meet," is outdated, outmoded and false in the face of what I have stated in this book. No attitude of provincialism and seclusion is possible today on the part of any country or culture. The world is willy-nilly heading towards a universal culture which transcends geographical and ideological limits. Values are the warp and woof of human culture and their study will help foster peace and understanding, perhaps even Arnold's "sweetness and light." Hence I will conclude this chapter by explaining the significance of economic, social, moral, and spiritual values, as briefly as possible.

The concept of value and the need of adhering to it are purely humane and are the distinctive marks of human life, as opposed to the instinctive and impulsive life of animals. In other words, the presence of value and the urge for moral life are entirely the outcome of the rationality of man, which makes him an economic animal, a social animal, and a tool-using animal. Man's moral and political organizations, his complicated economic structure and applied sciences and technology, are the outcome of the same urge of man which has given birth to the values of life, truth, beauty and goodness. But unfortunately in our science-ridden age of speed and motion, of unprecedented material advancement and technological research, which has resulted in man's mastery over time and space, an equal emphasis has not been laid on the exposition and significance of value, which is the coevolute of science. The disinterested search for truth by science and the adoption of this same indifferent method in the field of psychology, sociology and philosophy have resulted in the predominance of an attitude of skepticism and negativism in all fields of study in general and in philosophy in particular where it is least becoming. An academic attitude is understood and interpreted to mean an austere apathy towards human weal and woe, an abstract analytical thinking amounting to disregard of the needs of society and sometimes of hairsplitting and quibbling, irrespective of the futility of these ventures in the practical life of an oppressed humanity, which is thirsty for some positive ideal and constructive philosophy.

We have applied science to every walk of life and have unconsciously driven ourselves to believe that science is the be-all and the end-all of human culture and civilization, without at the same time realizing that we are committing the error of overlooking value, which is not only the co-product of science, from reason, but is also its complementary and compensating counterpart, without which neither science, nor art, nor society, nor religion, nor psychology, nor economics, nor commerce, nor law, nor logic, in short, nor human civilization, can ever flourish or be fostered in the world. This lack has led to a lopsided development of human personality, with the result that in the progressive societies, where science and technological research have raised the standards of living, the dangers of mental derangements, disrupted families, divorces on trivial grounds, callousness and unfriendliness toward human beings, and utter disregard of love and fellow feeling, have loomed large. Whereas science has taken long strides, ethics has lagged behind; science has been worshipped and has received adoration and unstinted devotion, morality has been pushed into the background. This is the main cause of the confusion and chaos which has led the contemporary world to the brink of committing nuclear suicide. It is in the face of these circumstances that the concept of value ought to be regarded as most significant from the economic, social and moral points of view, and that sociologists and philosophers should cast off their naturalistic bias and see that philosophy does not become the "handmaid of science" in our times, as it became the handmaid of religion in the middle ages. Contemporary society, in spite of being regarded as progressive, is most reactionary and conservative with regard to its tenacity in being the blind follower of science and the so-called scientific technique. Why should the results of science not be subjected to critical and rational estimation, and be harmonized with the value aspect of human nature? Science is the outcome of human nature and so is value; science is the symbol of human culture, and so is value. Science and morality, fact and value, and description and appreciation constitute the whole man and both exist because of man and for man.

Even if science were taken as the sole guide of all human activity, we cannot set aside the fact that human personality is one whole, and that it is not subject to atomic analysis so far as the understanding of human behavior is concerned. The contribution of the Gestalt, the psychoanalytic and existentialist schools of contemporary psychology have driven us to the conclusion that it is impossible to reduce human personality to the mechanical laws of causality, and that for the proper understanding of human psychology and human behavior we should never overlook the person as a whole, his physical, physiological makeup, his biological urges, his social, economic and spiritual motivation, and the interaction of heredity and environment, together with the unique dynamism of the human individual, which in spite of the acceptance of the continuity of the evolution of life, still marks him off as "the image of God" and "the crown of creation." If evolution is a process which is continuous and creative, the rational, self-conscious, appreciative, moral and spiritual aspects of man must have been somehow potentially present in the primaeval nebulae, and hence value, whether at the moral or at the spiritual level of human existence is not supernatural in the sense of being something, "beyond nature, behind nature and other than nature".

The need of adhering to economic, social, moral and spiritual values is demanded by the dynamic nature of man because he is a whole of the physico-biological, ethico-social and spirituo-rational urges. Since psychology in its recent researches has brought out the fact that a one-sided development of human personality is the cause of neuroses and mental diseases, it goes without saying that, psychologically speaking, equal attention to the integrated satisfaction of human urges is most important. It is from this point of view that I consider economic, social, moral and spiritual values to be of great significance in man's life. Economic values, which greatly influence the present structure of society in all parts of the world, are undoubtedly most important and even basic. No individual, no community, no nation can boast of being moral without adequately satisfying the physico-biological urges of men through the production of wealth, or economic value. A prosperous country, a country which has achieved economic well-being, automatically eliminates many social evils and wards off moral degeneration. This view of mine has been confirmed by my visits to America. The American people are honest workers, and hence evils like exploiting others by cheating, telling lies, or by conspiring, etc., are minimal as compared with less prosperous countries. India, in spite of its lofty idealism and rich spiritual heritage, cannot as a nation be said to be more ethical than America in this respect, because of its economic backwardness. The common man in America is more moral in this sense than the common man in India.

But the satisfaction of the physico-biological urges of man is not the end in itself. A philosophy of life which aims at equalizing or levelling down society economically, is not the answer to the integrated development of human personality. Human beings are not mere material product; minds cannot be lumped into one mass and made quantitatively equal and proportionate. Communism commits this fallacy in its attempt to bring about social well-being. But it defeats its purpose, with the result that it brings about suppression and regression instead of development and evolution. In a communistic regime where wealth alone is supposed to be the ultimate end of life, individual freedom of thought, feeling and action is thwarted, religion is relinquished, spiritualism is suppressed, the family is sacrificed and the individual reduced to a mere cog in the social machinery. In such a form of government natural growth of thought and culture are hampered, man is reduced to an automaton, life to a mechanical routine. Mind is subjected to matter, individual freedom to the laws of the commune, and parental affection towards children to the husbandry of the state.

Similarly extreme individualism and complete freedom in the economic field may lead to the concentration of wealth in a few persons, who grow extraordinarily rich and thus may keep an overwhelming majority of the people poor and frustrated, thereby fostering social evils. Owing to the prevailing poverty in underdeveloped democracies, the few rich persons can purchase votes and capture political power. They can monopolize trade and grow richer while the poor become poorer. All the abuses of wealth, overspending in luxuries, indulgence in intoxicants, etc., are likely to crop up. This happens when wealth alone is considered the highest value in a society. Ultimately ethical values are subordinated to the mad pursuit after wealth, and humanitarianism gives place to formalism. Art, literature, science, in short, the entire cultural fabric of the society and state may come under the sway of a plutocracy which corrupts man and curbs freedom. This economic slavery of man may spread gradually, and for centuries the people who fall victim to it may not even realize that their spirit is being subordinated to flesh and their conscience to callousness. Free enterprise raises the material standards of living by increasing the wants of the society, by providing every individual with all the amenities and comforts of life, and by giving him the opportunities to "eat, drink and be merry" even to the extent of drinking himself to death. But at the same time, it blunts the human spirit, murders morality, kills love, dismembers family life, disrupts social institutions and fosters fastidious divorces, split personalities, neuroses, complexes and suicides, thereby creating an unconscious hatred for man in the human mind. The outward glamor of life is accompanied by inner gloom in the mind of individuals. The need of the hour, therefore, is the emphasis on the checks and balances on the individual freedom and totalitarian tendencies. This can be done when equal attention is paid to the inculcation of economic, social, moral and spiritual values.

India laid down a scheme of life in the hoary past which originally aimed at the integrated development of the life of the individual and that of society. The four major values or ends of life propounded by the Indian seers declared the dignity of man and his potentiality to attain spiritual heights. These values, or the Purusharthas, were Artha, or wealth; Kama, or the satisfaction of desires; Dharma, or duty; and Moksha, or self realization. These four values correspond to the physico-biological, ethico-social, and spirituo-rational nature of man. Man according to the Indian viewpoint, is a complex whole of body, mind, reason and spirit, and hence the adoption of wealth for the development of the body, of love or the satisfaction of desires for the development of mind, morality or duty towards society for the development of rationality, and self-realization or intuitive enlightenment for the development of spirit was considered necessary to the integrated evolution of human personality. The main thesis of Indian thought and culture is the synthesis of the spiritual and the secular, of self-sacrifice and self-realization. India has produced spiritual giants who have in every age demonstrated the truth of applying the ideal of practical life and of bringing about a synthesis between ethics and metaphysics, science and religion, and of fact and value. They have again and again emphasized that the evolution of human personality is an ascent from the physical through the mental and rational to the heights of spirit. The physical body is controlled by mind, mental desires are controlled by reason and rationality is controlled by the spirit. This, however, obviously does not mean that economic and moral values are to be neglected. On the contrary, this view points out that by adopting spiritual discipline in life the integrated development of body, mind, reason and spirit is possible and that such a development is not antagonistic to the material and mundane progress of mankind. Thus the present need is a serious study of the intuitive method of approach, so far as the value aspect of human life is concerned, without at the same time jeopardizing the analytic method in the sphere of science and facts. A synthesis of intellect and intuition, of science and ethics, and of secular and spiritual life can lead to the emergence of a world culture which would be through and through a human culture. This can be accomplished by laying an equal emphasis on economic, social, moral, and spiritual values in human life.

DUE